STARSTRUCK IN LODI AGAIN

STARSTRUCK IN LODI AGAIN

Lodi Wine Country

CHRIS KASSEL

Photography by Randy Caparoso, Sean Piper and Chris Kassel

Paperback Edition
First Printing July 2016

ISBN-13: 978-1535167130
ISBN-10: 1535167130
BISAC: Travel / United States / West / General

CONTENTS

FOREWORD, Not by John Fogerty..I

1. LODI–I'M TOKAY, YOU'RE TOKAY.......................................1

2. THE WIZARD OF OZV: RUDY MAGGIO HAS YOU UNDER A BARREL...........13

3. PAUL SCOTTO AND A GLEAM IN HIS OLD MAN'S EYE...................21

4. CALLING THE SCHATZ FROM A THOUSAND FEET.......................33

5. JOHN 'THE GURU' MCCLELLAND: LAST OF THE OLD GUARD..............39

6. LIFE IN THE TALL LAYNE: m2 WINES.............................47

7. MIKE MCCAY IS THE REAL MCCOY................................53

8. A3'S NOT YELLING–HE'S EXCITED...............................57

9. THE ALEXANDERS AND THE REINCARNATION OF PYTHAGORAS............63

10. 'ACQUIESCE' MEANS 'ACCEPT WITHOUT PROTEST'...................71

11. THE HOUSE THAT CESARE BUILT................................81

12. NATALIE SCOTTO: STREAMLINING THE LEVIATHAN.................87

13. ESTATE CRUSH: NEGATING THE NEGATIVE........................93

14. MOHR-FRY IS NOT A FAST FOOD ORDER.........................101

15. MARKUS NIGGLI: NOUVEAU NICHE..............................107

16. THE FLUID PRICELESS AND KEYS TO THE KINGDOM 115

17. SHAWN THE FLOP AND AL THE WOP.............................121

18. MICHAEL SCOTTO: NEVER THE WEAKEST LINK....................129

19. LA SABROSITA AND THE A&Ω OF A&W...........................133

20. MICHAEL DAVID AND THE NAME THAT LAUNCHED A THOUSAND QUIPS...139

21. THE CREEPIEST SPOT IN LODI................................145

22. A2: THE SYNDICATE OF FATE.................................153

23. HOME BEACONS: LEAVING LODI................................163

STARSTRUCK IN LODI AGAIN

Lodi Wine Country

FOREWORD

By the time I learned that Lodi was going to be the host city for the *2016 Wine Bloggers Conference* I had already started a book about the place, so I considered the news a stroke of fortune. In fact, I had already settled on a title—an excruciating pun (of course) on the John Fogerty song from 1969.

And shortly after I learned that Lodi was going to host the conference, somebody quipped, "Great, now we'll have to read five hundred blogs with titles that are puns on that stupid Fogerty song."

That hurt, and I quickly saw that I had few professional options. I could change the book title of course, or I could get the thing published before the five hundred blogs came out, thus earning bragging rights for having led the pack down the most obvious course. But my optimal choice, while difficult, seemed brilliant: I could track down John Fogerty himself and score an interview—even a brief one—during which I could ask him why he wrote the tune in the first place.

I could then transcribe the response as a 'Foreword'; thus lending my excruciating Lodi pun some creedence.

Before I continue, allow me clear up some misconceptions. First, in my world, *'Lodi'* isn't a particularly stupid song—I happen to dig it. Second, the only way most people ABC (Anywhere But California) have even *heard* of Lodi is through Fogerty's plaintive four-chord dirge about being stuck there. Writers tend to operate on mind associations, and had it not been for *'Lodi'* (which I learned to play pretty early in my brief cover-band career) I probably would not have been as interested in learning more about her reputation as stellar wine country. Did 'stuck' refer to fermentation? Was 'while people sat there drunk' a reference to tasting rooms?

Only John Fogerty could answer those questions, of course—or so I figured. And then, in the course of due-diligence, I discovered that according to Fogerty's bio, he has never even *been* to Lodi and only chose the town name because it sounded sort of lonely and cool and fit the meter of the lyrics.

But before that solar plexus blow could dampen my trouper's resolve, I found another quote from Fogerty's then-drummer, Doug Clifford. Clear as water is Clifford's recollection of the proto-Creedence band The Golliwogs (composed of himself, Fogerty and Stu Cook on piano), playing a series of one-night stands in small California towns throughout the mid-Sixties, and Lodi was among them:

"There were nine people in there, they were all locals, they were all drunk and all they did all night was tell us to turn it down."

In some phantom radio interview, Fogerty is said to have mentioned camping at Lodi Lake as a child, but I couldn't find a recording of it and in any case, that wouldn't explain the dystopian funk that the song's protag finds himself in. Let's be honest: Doesn't that more closely resembles Doug Clifford's memory revival?

This isn't the first time that Clifford and Fogerty have a different version of things, either. In a mega-dollars legal rift that rivals that of former Lodi luminaries Robert and Peter Mondavi, after Creedence Clearwater Revival broke up in 1972, Fogerty traded his rights to his own CCR songs in exchange for cancelling his remaining contractual obligations. In 1985, Saul Zaentz (who then owned the copyrights) sued Fogerty over his tune *'Old Man Down The Road'* because he claimed it sounded too much like *'Run Through the Jungle'*, which Fogerty also wrote, making Fogerty the only performer I can think of who has ever been sued for plagiarizing himself.

Clifford and Fogerty wrangled in court again in 1997 after Clifford (along with Stu Cook) began touring as 'Creedence Clearwater Revisited'. Fogerty briefly forced the band to change their name, but ultimately the court decided in Clifford's favor and 'Revisited' tours to this day.

The upshot? In the end, I had to punt. There will be no explanatory, revelatory, cathartic Fogerty Foreword to this tome, because, despite many attempts, the best feedback I could get from Richard De La Font Booking (John Fogerty's agency-of-record) was a price list.

As long as De La Font determines that I am a 'legitimate journalist' and not just some random fan looking to score a chat, the price for a ten minute interview with John Fogerty is $10,000.

Now, if I had that kind of cash, I wouldn't be stuck in Lodi writing a book about being stuck in Lodi, would I? So that leaves me with my final option:

Writing a Foreword *about* John Fogerty and anticipating a call, if not from his agent, at least from his attorney (!)

– Chris Kassel, June, 2016

1. LODI—I'M TOKAY, YOU'RE TOKAY

Miami bears the burden of an unfortunate nickname: *'God's Waiting Room—Where Old Folks Go to Die'*.

If that's the case, South School Street is where old folks go to Lodi. At any given moment, from about six in the morning to nine at night, there is a knot of pensioners mixing it up and mingling it down in front of the Lodi Hotel, directly across the street from the window in the apartment where I'm ensconced.

The 'LH' was once the most significant hotel in San Joaquin County, playing host to major social events, important business meetings and those snooty club dinners that have traditionally separated the haves from the have-nots in rural America. Today, it is a run-down-looking senior living community catering exclusively to the have-nots, where rooms go for $400 a month and most residents look like they are on

1

the downside of long lives. They can be seen coming and going with tattered backpacks and rickety walking canes throughout the day and smoking cigars and hobnobbing until well into the night. These are not particularly desperate-looking people—just oldsters doing their final, convivial nods to fate.

Demographically, the Lodi population over the age of 65 is considerably higher than the average in California, and a major part of the Lodi wine renaissance goal is to attract a younger, hipper crowd to this downtown area. But, we'll get to that.

My first inkling that Lodi culture was a bit unique came on Superbowl Sunday when I went in search of a sports bar to watch this over-hyped, over-rated, but still obligatory advertising fest. I had just landed in town as a total stranger, but I assumed I could find a sports bar; this is Warriors country, and there is an almost rabid support of the local high school basketball team 'The Flames'—a name I will explain shortly. But shockingly, the downtown brewpub was locked, nearly all the restaurants were closed, and when I finally tripped over Porter's Pub with its eight wide-screen televisions, I found fewer customers than TVs.

The bartender explained it like this: "In Lodi, Superbowl Sunday is a family day, not a bar day. People are at home."

Like the denizens gathered in front of the Lodi Hotel, the fans at Porter's Pub were retired folks, probably (like me) with no families to descend upon. On a balmy Sunday afternoon in February, with nowhere else to go and the underdog kicking ass on the 50" Vizio overheads, we commiserated.

So, the Lodi Flames (a name you suspect subjected them to endless taunts from the troglodytes) took their handle from the Flame Tokay grape, such a significant part of Lodi's economic history that reminders of it appear everywhere, on billboards, on store logos, on magazine covers. There's Tokay High School, there's Tokay Cold Storage, Tokay Heating & Air Conditioning, Tokay Medical Billing, Tokay Food & Liquor... *et cetera.*

Lodi is currently the epicenter of California's Old Vine Zinfandel industry, and yet, in downtown Lodi, all the conspicuous homage is paid to the Flame Tokay, a grape that was not used in wine production at all, unless you count a few sparkling wines from years gone by, due more to abundance than advisability. Although it is a mutant version of the Algerian *Vitis vinifera* varietal Ahmeur Bou'Ahmeur, it has been almost universally marketed as a table grape.

At one time, Flame Tokay was Lodi's dominant cash crop, critical to the agricultural economy.

The Flame Tokay earns its own name from the vibrant reddish hue it draws from the iron rich soils of San Joaquin County, where hot days give over to cold nights—a terroir not precisely duplicated elsewhere. In Sacramento, for example, fifty miles north, Tokay does not flame. In many ways, the reverence Lodi displays for the Tokay grape—unrelated to Alsace Tokay, by the way, which is Pinot Gris, nor Hungarian Tokaji, which is a blend of grapes, primarily Furmint—is perfectly understandable: Lodi is the house that Tokay built, and vice versa.

The only problem is, they don't grow it any more.

In the early part of the twentieth century, Flame Tokay was among the most popular table grapes on the American market, but it had one major drawback: Seeds. When seedless grapes were developed in the 1970s, demand dropped almost immediately, and today, the vast majority of table grapes grown in California are *sin semilla*—seed free—and the majority of those are Thompson, cultivated primarily as a raisin grape.

Thompson does not require Lodi's signature diurnal temperature shift to develop desirable qualities; wine grapes do to preserve acids and Flame Tokay does to make all the pretty colors. A seedless version of Tokay was quickly bred, and that's what dropped the other shoe: It turned out that Flame Seedless could be grown more cheaply and more effectively in hot, dry Thompson terrain.

Today, there is such scant demand for Lodi-style Flame Tokay that San Joaquin County's Agricultural Commissioner's office doesn't even track how many acres are left; with over a hundred thousand Lodi acres planted to vine, probably less than 500 of them are Flame Tokay. During the glory days of peak production, Flame Tokay was a hundred times more abundant, with half a million acres planted.

Meanwhile, today more than 40% of California's Zinfandel hails from Lodi, and with 20,000 acres currently dedicated to it, it is by far the dominant varietal. With vineyards averaging a hundred acres, a random drive through the agricultural spread of San Joaquin County reveals a seemingly endless expanse of Old Vine Zinfandel—field after field of gnarled, angry-looking stumps which by mid-February have been pruned to something resembling miniature Christmas trees after a forest fire. Without foliage, they are ugly and fascinating, twisted and savage, fierce enough to almost look like they're in pain.

For all the world, these venerable vines look like the old dudes in wheelchairs killing hours outside the Lodi Hotel. And the incinerated-look analogy may be more apt than originally intended: If Satan has a vineyard, I imagine it looks a lot like OVZ.

The funny thing is, in the fly-over state where I live, 'Old Vine Zinfandel' sounds like something rare, unique and utterly exotic—some elixir arising from a handful of still-surviving vines that have been around so long they are producing small, concentrated clusters of sensational wine grapes. I suppose we are easy to impress. Here in Lodi, from a cursory glance, Old Vine Zinfandel is all there seems to be; at least, there doesn't appear to be much New Vine Zinfandel. In field after field, farm after farm, vineyard after vineyard, I see three distinct stages of Zinfandel's useful life: Old, older and Bernie Sanders.

There's even an abandoned Old Zin vineyard in the middle of town, unkempt, unharvested, but still very much alive.

And yet, cruise around the city itself, and do you know how many Zinfandel Cold Storage or Zinfandel Medical Billing storefronts you'll see? Zero. Zip. Zilch.

It's a slow, sleepy, hidebound ag town, very much the opposite of the place described in the opening line of Yeats' poem *Sailing to Byzantium*: Lodi—for now anyway—is very much a country for old men. And old vines.

Wine's history here is also old; in fact, Lodi has been a paradise for vines since before Lodi was even Lodi. The first Europeans arrived in the area 1846 and named the settlement along the banks of the Mokelumne River exactly that: The Mokelumne Settlement. By 1874, confusion with the nearby communities of Mokelumne Hill and Mokelumne City became an issue, particularly with mail deliveries and shipped goods, and the founding fathers renamed the town 'Lodi', most likely in tribute to Napoleon's Italian Waterloo: The battle of Lodi, 1796. The city was incorporated in 1904, and by that time, the wine grape industry was in full swing.

Flame Tokay was a big part of the original boom, but by the turn of the twentieth century, Zinfandel and Carignane were also thriving. In fact, 95% of the vines at Bechthold Vineyard today are from that era, and some are even older. Prior to the century's turn, San Joaquin Valley had followed various farmer's markets as prices rose and fell; a consistent topography with 50 to 150-ft. elevation flats and less than 2% slopes—along with an enormous aquifer, ideal climate and fertile soil— saw virtually every crop they attempted flourish. It's one of those 'throw the seeds and run like hell' agricultural Arcadias, and at one time, San Joaquin Valley produced the largest wheat crop on the planet. When the wheat prices fell, they tried watermelon, and suddenly, by 1900, San Joaquin was *'Watermelon Capital of the World'*.

Interestingly, the phylloxera blight in the late nineteenth century that was to California grapes what the Black Death was to European peasants skipped over Lodi like a stone across the Camanche Reservoir. That's because the miserable little root louse that ate Napa and Sonoma does not proliferate in the sandy soils around Lodi, and although the Bechthold acres are the oldest Lodi vineyards still producing, there are plenty of vines in the vicinity that are still fecund on ungrafted root stock.

So these are old vines with an old history growing on old rootstock in an old community where the old folks hang out in front of an old hotel.

Notice a theme that dominates that observation?

Randy Caparoso does; he's a major flag-waver for changes that are happening in the region. A long time wine journalist and sommelier, he was *Sante Magazine's* first 'Wine & Spirits Professional of the Year' (1998) and he has personally opened more than twenty upscale restaurants located from Honolulu to New York. Originally based in Orange County, he was convinced that something majestic was happening in Lodi following a series of mind-blowing wines he tasted from an AVA he had previously considered, "Merely an extension of the hot, irrigated desert of the Central Valley."

His watershed moment came during the late Jerry Mead's *New World Wine Competition 2003* when he and the other judges unanimously awarded "Best of Show" to a beautifully balanced, organeptically-extraordinary Syrah that wound up being a 2000 Delicato Shiraz. Randy was so impressed by it that he tried to get his hands on a quantity of unbottled wine from Delicato's next vintage to blend with his own self-described "uninteresting" cache of Cabernet Sauvignon, custom-crushed from Paso Robles fruit for his private label. The blend brightened up his wine, his day and his subsequent outlook, and the more he learned about the quality transition that was then beginning to envelop Lodi (largely through the efforts of the Lodi Winegrape Commission), the more impressed he became. He wound up moving to Lodi in 2010.

"The microclimate here is remarkable," he maintains. "It's almost like growing grapes on the east side of Sonoma or in the Napa Valley. Modesto is forty miles away, but it's twice as hot. Lodi is in a whole different growing zone."

Modesto may not be twice as hot, but Lodi is certainly cooled from steady breezes from the San Joaquin/Sacramento River Delta, leaving it with a classic Mediterranean climate. Annual rainfall is in the range of 17 inches a fraction of that in Southern Rhône and Bordeaux, but it mostly comes during the winter months so that the growing season is a Goldilocks set of viticultural conditions: Warm, dry days and cool nights, ideal for reducing pest and disease issues while allowing grapes to achieve a complete ripeness of tannins and phenolics with natural acidity remaining intact. Irrigation is key, and nobody around here even whispers the term ⊠dry farmed⊠.

The demand for Lodi's cash cow table grape evaporated at around the same time that Americans were discovering that there were a few superb wines made in California and floating in some obscurity buoy upon the sea of bulk that dominated the supermarkets of Middle America. So when Lodi growers were looking to replace the vast acres of Flame Tokay, many of them looked to the success stories in Napa and figured they had a shot at emulating them based on a terroir that was not dissimilar.

In fact, an inconvenient truth that the big names in Napa do not like advertised to this day is that many of their most sanctified selections have traditionally contained juice from Lodi—and in some cases, a lot of juice from Lodi. TBB law stipulates that to window-dress your label with an appellation name like Napa, or with an even tighter sub-appellation name like Howell Mountain, only 75% of that wine must originate there, leaving vintners with a whopping margin for blending richer, less expensive, often superior grapes from elsewhere. Often, that winds up being Lodi, where a ton of quality fruit may be ten times cheaper than its Napa counterpart.

Naturally, the finished wine with the fancy 'Napa' on the label still commands a fancy Napa price.

Even Lodi people walk a thin line when admitting this, even though everybody knows it. Figure that a lot of Lodi growers owe their very existence to Napa/Sonoma sales, and pissing off the boss is not always a good career move.

According to Randy, "It's generally considered impolite to talk about certain things that might burst people's bubble. Most of what is grown in Lodi supplies the big industrial producers, and business is successfully done with some degree of discretion. If your Aunt Agatha is crazy or your Uncle Bud is in a closet, why scream it out to the rest of the world just to show you know?"

Whereas I respect Randy's ethics, the fact of the matter is that I am in the business of telling honest stories where chips may not always fall where the subjects like, and for me, the nuttier Aunt Agatha or Uncle Bud are, the better. Nothing about, say, Lucian Freud, Francis Bacon or Eric Fischl to me seems more intriguing than the idea that the dynamism of their style may have actually been the work of apprentices and assistants operating in a factory-like setting.

In any case, when the bleak light of Life-After-Flame-Tokay shone on Lodi's vineyards, the brave new world was not going to be found in bulk wine sales to Gallo or Constellation, where their own contribution—however indispensable—was drowned in a deluge of Napa names or Sonoma sobriquets:

It lay in pushing their own brand to the head of the class.

The first step to that end was seeing the appellation established, and in 1986, the northern edge of the San Joaquin Valley east of San Francisco Bay gained approval as a designated wine growing area, including 551,000 acres of land, of which 103,000 acres are currently planted with wine grapes. In 2002, the Lodi AVA was expanded by 93,500 acres along the southern and western portions of the original boundaries. This gave the Lodi Winegrape Commission something tangible to sink their promotional teeth into, and a starting point through which to develop a genuine commercial interest in the region that reflected the value of the crop.

The growers in Lodi were on board immediately. Many of them had been in the area for generations and intend to remain here for many more; thus, they look at mindset transitions and paradigm shifts in terms of decades, not years. The core of any sustainable agricultural philosophy is respect for the land, so when the Commission began to solicit ideas from farmers and wineries to improve the quality not only of Lodi wine, but the quality of Lodi life, an overview known as 'The Lodi Rules' was the outcome.

In a Cliff's Notes version, The Lodi Rules are a series of standards designed to promote sustainable viticulture. There are 101 of them, covering such topics as business management, human resources, ecosystems, soil management, water and pest management, and it lead to a rigorous science-based, voluntary and third-party-audited certification program.

Says Caparoso, "The Lodi Rules launched in 2006, and it quickly became a blueprint for sustainable ag programs all over California. You'll find our book with a different cover and a few details changed to custom fit various other appellations, all over the place. The origins are right here. More than 26,000 winegrape acres have now been certified in California so far."

Taking the idea up another notch, Caparoso calls himself ⊠the den mother⊠ of a second forward leap within the Lodi quality scene: The Lodi Native Project. Launched as a wine label in 2012, the mission of six Lodi winemakers was to release collaborative wines that focused on individual vineyard terroirs, long a hallmark of quality in wine regions around the world. The spotlight is on heritage Zinfandel plantings, some from the 1880s, and the goal is to produce pure, unmanipulated Zinfandel that reflects the unique site upon which it is grown. Like the Lodi Rules, the Native project has its own set of protocols, including a mandate that only native yeast can be used in fermentation, that there can be no artificial adjustment of acid levels or any dilution or must concentration, Flash Détente or similar extraction measures and the wine must be aged in neutral barrels in order to preserve the essence of the terroir.

Besides being a purist's paradisiacal prototype, according to Caparoso, there's a marketing angle to producing Old Vine Zin according to Lodi Native rules:

"Too much Old Vine Zinfandel is vinified in an over-the-top, bigger-is-better Parker style. They tend to rely on maximum extraction from ultra ripe fruit, and wind up being statement wines—not particularly elegant. Not particularly food-friendly, either, and in general, sommeliers and chefs don't like them. San Francisco is one thing, but look at an upscale wine list from any high-market restaurant in Chicago or New York and if you see any Old Vine Zinfandel, it's a placeholder; a concession rather than a recommendation. So the intention of Lodi Native is to craft wines that a sommelier can love; a non-manipulated, un-doctored wine that shows off another side of the varietal—a nuanced side; the natural expression of the grape."

Throughout my stay, I have engaged in my own Lodi Native Project, seeking out the non-manipulated and the un-doctored among Lodi's citizens. I've chatted with the old guys sitting in the sun in front of the hotel, I've rubbed shoulders with up-by-the bootstraps dudes who at any given time have a million gallons of wine ready to bottle with another hundred thousand bottles on store shelves throughout the world. I've run with those who made their own fortunes and those who inherited them; I've dealt with Lodi boosters of all ages, all professions, all stripes.

The dudes at the top of the food chain are easy enough to track down—they're rightly proud of their achievements and are more than willing to display it in a single encompassing overview from the cockpit of their private airplanes.

But the bottom of the food chain is equally accessible, equally open: In the alley behind my temporary apartment on S. School there's a young man named Shawn. He's been homeless for five years, living beneath a discarded-mattress-tent for the last two. He's hardly the only indigent, but he's one of the few African Americans of any social station—Lodi's black population is less than 1%. I bring Shawn cigarettes (my bad) and roast chickens (my good) and at least once a day, rap with him for a while about the state of the whole metaphysical scenario—he's a little cosmic and spacey, which probably explains his living arrangements.

Nevertheless, he is as solidly entrenched in my story—Lodi's story—as the dirt farmers who went from dirt poor to filthy rich overnight when (thanks to the White Zinfandel craze of the '80s) the price of their crop skyrocketed from $200 per ton to $1200 per ton. Shawn is an example of the Lodites who, for a multitude of reasons as complex as the nose on a 2000 Delicato Shiraz, were left behind.

I spent a month with a special set of aggressive, determined Lodi folks who were not left behind; in fact, they built the railroad. It was a journey with a few bumps and handful of bruises, and the pages that follow are the chronicle of the best of them:

I encourage you hop on board and grab a berth.

2. THE WIZARD OF OZV: RUDY MAGGIO HAS YOU UNDER A BARREL

A pastoral phenomenon known as 'fairy rings' has a long history among bards and dreamers; they're circular rings of mushrooms that may grow to thirty feet in diameter. Folklore tells us that they are places where pixies dance; mycologists assure us that it is the result of mycelium expanding outward as they deplete nutrients in the soil.

There is a wine equivalent to fairy rings, and they can be seen quite elegantly on the floor of Woodbridge Beverage Company on E. Victor Road in Lodi. This massive, sagging, desperately picturesque structure is one of those solid old places that you drive by in the countryside and have fun imagining its history. Only in this case, I didn't drive by—I stopped and went inside and learned the history.

Woodbridge Beverage Company (not to be confused with nearby Woodbridge Winery, a Constellation powerhouse) is home to Scotto

Family Cellars' Villa Armando Vino Rustico brand, and it certainly plays the rustic role to the hilt. Everything looks venerable, which is a polite word for old, and everything smells like a few decades worth of wine.

The office houses Dana, who sends out the reviewer sample packages through which I first discovered Scotto Family Cellars; it's a nerve center, no question, but not necessarily the first place you bring corporate wine buyers. Everything here is held together with thumbtacks and duct tape; the chairs are in tatters, the furniture is garage sale, the walls made out of particle board and K-Mart paneling and the floor is littered with little white dots, the detritus of several generations' worth of paper punching

Still, the entire shebang—paper dots, *Mystery Spot, Santa Cruz* bumper sticker on the wall, leaky heaving concrete floors, old scraggly vines like witch's hair festooning the old red brick outside—is the place where Anthony Scotto II—henceforth referred to as 'A2'—hangs his hat. It's the place where, in his own words, he feels most comfortable:

"These are our roots," he says.

There are a million stories connected with this building, and a lot of them have the word 'million' in them. Leaving out the dollar signs, this place used to hold a million gallons of wine, and when A2 dismantled the redwood fermenters, he wound up with a million board feet of hundred-year-old clear heart redwood planks, fifty years old. It took him two years to sell it to contractors, mostly for hot tubs, decks and molding for the houses of millionaires.

The huge redwood fermenters, a century old and capable of holding 80,000 gallons each, left an indelible imprint on the concrete floor—a ghost image, a fairy ring. Leakage from the wine, highly acidic, has eaten into the alkaline cement and left large circles where the tanks once stood.

Directly across the street from Woodbridge Beverage Company one of those tanks remains intact, and now serves as a kitschy, if charming tasting room for Oak Ridge Wines. I peeked in, but my *mano a mano tête à tête* was in the small office next door, where I sat for an hour with Rudy Maggio, one of the genuine characters in the local wine scene, a Lodi original.

Maggio is one of those dudes that journalists used to describe as a 'fireplug'—short, stocky, big-bellied and tough as nails. In the event that your mind has been wandering, his is the kind of handshake that brings you back to earth. He's Lodi born and raised and his accent reflects it, mostly in the pronunciation of the 'o' in dollar or college, which comes out more the 'o' in bought, at least to my Midwestern ear.

The Maggio clan has had several generations to hone that 'o.' The family patriarch, Angelo, emigrated to California from Rapallo, Italy in 1906, the year of the earthquake. He had a farm job in Stockton awaiting him, but found steadier work among the cleanup crews who were working in the ruins of downtown San Francisco. By 1910, his future wife's family had come over from Luca, Italy; Angelo married, and in 1913, Rudy's father was born. By the late 1920s, the Maggios had purchased 200 hundred acres of Lodi grapeland: This was the height of Prohibition, so the land was inexpensive and the primary market was in shipping Mission and Zinfandel grapes east on rail cars chilled with ice blocks.

Special permits allowed the manufacture of sacramental wines for Catholic church services and bricks of dried grapes were sold along with packets of yeast bearing the warning label against adding water and leaving it in the cupboard for seven days, in which case 'an illegal alcoholic beverage might result'. But more money was made through a loophole in the Volstead Act of 1920 which allowed home winemakers to 'bathtub gin' up to 200 gallons per year, and at the peak of production, Maggio's family was shipping 200 boxcars of wine grapes annually. This was before the advent of mechanical refrigeration, and the cars had a special compartment in the bulkheads, which were loaded with ice and had fans that operated by the motion of the wheels. This was the preferred method of moving product long after Prohibition ended; the family switched to shipping via trucks in the 1950s and shipped their last truckload of wine grapes in 1980.

After that, there was no real need—like many Lodi growers, the local market for wine grapes was exploding, and Rudy Maggio—by then a leader among local grape growers, was experimenting with various agricultural improvements that were required as the market for California table wine expanded. Then, as now, there were plenty of old Zinfandel vines in Lodi, and this was an integral part of what made Gallo's legendary, albeit misnamed 'Hearty Burgundy'. If you can find a serious review of this wine written by a serious critic—and you probably can't—you'll see that the tasting notes have a lot in common with a review of any Old Vine Zinfandel and for reasons I assume are now obvious.

The explosive popularity of simplistic, eminently quaffable White Zinfandel in the last decades of the twentieth century had far more of an impact on Lodi grape growers than classic OVZ, of course—it outsells red zin by a margin of ten to one, and accounts for around 10% of the entire American wine market. Like many Lodi growers, the economic belt-tightening of the '80s was reaching critical mass mid-decade, and Rudy was a hair's breadth from going under when the price of Zinfandel-by-the-ton began to rise. The two thousand tons that might normally have sold for a couple hundred bucks suddenly became worth a thousand per ton to Gallo and Franzia, and he went from bankruptcy to buying Boardwalk overnight.

The infusion of working capital allowed the operation to begin the move from furrowed ditches with sulphur sacks as dams to drip irrigation and mechanical harvesting; meanwhile, Rudy Maggio sat on the board at Oak Ridge Winery, which was—in his words—"Spending too much time trying to sell wine and not enough time making it."

In 2002, along with a couple partners, Rudy Maggio took the winery's reins, and as he did when he upgraded his vineyards, he set to work improving the brand, the image, the quality and the export potential. You can check off each item off as 'mission accomplished'. Although Oak Ridge is the oldest operating winery in Lodi, it is today a state-of-the-art facility with multiple labels, many accolades and is insanely popular in—of all places—Sweden.

Equally unlikely as a Swedish base is the fact that Rudy shares a portion of Oak Ridge's success to a winemaker named Chue. Chue Her, who—by virtue of probably being the only native Laotian winemaker on the planet—amps the 'unlikely' level further skyward. When I asked Chue what his parents thought of him going into the wine business, he shook his head in imitation of their apparent bewilderment: "They wanted me to be a pharmacist."

Chue studied chemistry in college, and still managed to find a pharmacopeia of a different sort; he has a cocky sort of self-confidence in his approach to winemaking and claims that if you hand him a bottle of any wine in the world, he can come up with a very close approximation using Lodi fruit, relying on chemical analyses to isolate various profiles relating to residual sugar, pH, titratable acidity and other such requisites.

Chue Her

And that's not as far-fetched as it might seem: Distributors are asking for this kind of hocus-pocus from wineries all the time. For example, they might request a brand that tastes exactly like Kenall-Jackson Chardonnay (among the top-selling wines in history) but costs a couple bucks less. Chue name-drops a couple of his other success stories, but I probably shouldn't mention them. In any case, at the core of his winemaking philosophy is succinctly stated: "I don't believe that a wine enthusiast should have to pay more than $50 for any bottle of wine. Above a certain point, the price on the bottle is rarely the best measurement of the quality of the wine inside."

Back in the tasting room, the signature wine goes by the name 'OZV', which is Old Vine Zinfandel for dyslexics. It reflects both the heritage and the vigor of the Maggio's vineyard management and winemaking; the 2014 vintage took a silver medal in the most recent San Francisco

Chronicle Wine Competition.

Yet, the winery's OZV Rosé may in fact be a better epitome for the cause: Despite being a gussy-upped name for White Zinfandel, that's exactly what it is, of course. It's a quality version of the stuff that originated here (George West of El Pinal Winery made the first White Zin ever in Lodi in 1869) and—true to the Chue view—sells for fourteen dollars at BevMo. That pales in comparison to the accolade the wine received at the most rustic-sounding, plebian-pleasing, down-home wine competition of them all:

2014 OZV Rosé was named Class Champion at Houston Livestock/ Rodeo & International Wine Competition 2016.

Barrel racing is one of rodeo's top events. Roll out it out, Rudy: We'll have a barrel of fun.

3: PAUL SCOTTO AND A GLEAM IN HIS OLD MAN'S EYE

Last August I wrote a piece about tasting a slew of sensational ciders with Paul Scotto in a motel room in Corning, New York, and—wannabe stand-up comic that I am—I prefaced it like this:

'If the most exciting thing that's happened to you in a motel room this year has been tasting cider with Paul Scotto, welcome to my world...'

Rimshot, huh? *Tish bang?* Except that six months later, where did I end up—dateless—on Valentine's Day? Tasting ciders with Paul Scotto in some restaurant in Danville, California.

Suddenly, it isn't so funny anymore.

At least this time Paul brought along his wife, the incomparably lovely Whitney Colli Scotto, who began as a farm girl from Santa Maria who fell for Paul at first sight and vice versa. Now three children into it, she still manages to exude such wholesome farm-girl radiance that the old

Arthur Fields song worried about *keepin' down on the farm* is much ado about nothing: They'll do just fine, Art.

Paul's younger sister Bianca and his mother Gracie were doing tag-team babysitting that evening so that he and his wife could spend an intimate Valentine's Day together—just them and me and a table-load of groupies eager to hear the Cider Brothers' back story and tuck into incarnations of Red Dragon Ciders paired with cutting-edge California cuisine at The Growler Pub in Danville.

Speaking of 'tuck', a couple of words on that word should be sufficient: Paul Scotto's other cider brand is 'William Tell', and he's launching a campaign to explain the origin of the name—which refers to the legendary Swiss folk hero who shot an apple off his kid's head. The campaign is called *Who The Hell Is William Tell?'* and as such, the whole marketing department thanks its (possessive) stars that the dude's name wasn't William Tuck.

Anyway, Growler Pub's executive chef is a self-described 'beer girl' named Rachel Zavala, and when called upon to become a cider girl when planning the Valentine's Day menu, acquitted herself magnificently. She was kind enough to explain in culinary detail her food and cider pairing decision, and I'll offer some Zavala sound bites related to each course:

"The straight, unflavored dry Red Dragon cider matched well with Asparagus Soup; the floral smoky quality cut through the Parmesan Custard."

"Ale yeast was used in the cider/Pinot Grigio blend, and this gave it a nutty warmth and a creaminess that I thought went perfectly with Lardo-Wrapped Prawns with Grapefruit Chips and Hazelnut Gremolata."

"Cherry Cider brought with it a complex, seafood-friendly quality that balanced the Lemon-Rosemary Stuffed Branzino and the dry vanilla notes

went nicely with the Steak Diane."

"*Finally, the Strawberry cider completed the traditional Valentine's Day duo of strawberries and chocolate, which is why I paired it with Flourless Chocolate Cake and Caramel Ice Cream.*"

This was an interesting California Dreamin' experience, and the fact that Chef Rachel announced before and after the meal that it was gluten free and the fact that Red Dragon Cider also advertises that it is gluten free, initially struck me as the same sort of ironic joke that had me in a pub with strangers on Valentine's Day two thousand miles from home. Didn't we all sort of collectively agree that gluten isn't particularly bad for you unless you are among the 1% of the population with a wheat allergy? And isn't beer, the bevvie upon which the Growler builds it fan base pretty gluten-dependent? As a boy from the grain belt, I was not aware that the anti-gluten movement was still alive and kicking on the Left Coast; I thought the idea that a gluten-less lifestyle was healthier had been relegated to the Snopes-heap of busted fad diets.

I'd say, "Bring on the barley and pasta," except that Chef Rachel's menu was so spectacular that I didn't miss a gram of gluten anywhere along the trail.

Paul Scotto's cider may be California-friendly, but his raw material is not from California. He now bottles and cans so much of it that the Lodi apple orchards can't possibly keep up. Today, he brings it in by the tanker load from Washington, 5,500 gallons at a time.

It was not necessarily an operation intended to grow so quickly and exponentially: As Paul tells it, it was a mere three years ago that he began to play around with fresh apple juice, sensing that the U.S. market for fermented cider was about to do a post-*Sideways* Pinot Noir. In fact, he was right: Cider has represented one of the most WTF? sales

23

trajectories in craft beverage history. There are as many explanations for that as there are cider buffs, and most of the analyses refer to cider as a gender-neutral beverage, a flavor-of-the-month for trendapoids, a heritage beverage that hearkens us back to our colonial history. But they all can be consolidated into a single bullet point:

Hard cider is scrumptious—one of the easiest beverages ever concocted for a grownup to love.

Not everybody has instantly climbed aboard the apple cart, and an example involves a respected Napa winemaker whose name I will, with some struggle, avoid mentioning. He recently dissed a bottle of William Tell Cider (untasted) by likening it to 7-Up with a shot of vodka. I responded that it's not particularly sweet, not particularly alcoholic and distinctly un-artificial tasting. Then I was forced to remind him that Scotto's cider is not attempting to compete with the sort of $85 Napa Cabs he makes, and that a lot of $85 Napa Cabs—including a few of his—are severely overpriced.

Nobody can say that William Tell is a rip-off at $9 for 22 oz., at least, not with a straight face.

The final cider formula upon which Paul settled took a bit of time, but not as much as you might think: By the time he considered cider, he'd already cut his teeth as Scotto Family Cellars' vintner, and, as he is the first to admit, cider is an easier beast to tackle.

Big bro Anthony takes credit for the original idea of having Paul craft "a refreshing drink lighter than beer, less potent than wine and reliant on a spritz of fizz to appeal to a coed crowd at, say, a weekend cookout." If there was any downside of such a brainstorm, Anthony shrugs, "I'm not sure how many batches he tried, because I nearly burned out tasting the experiments." But in February, 2014, he nailed it. His ciders have the same subtleties and complexities as some of his award-winning wines, and at 6% ABV, this something you can drink all afternoon."

Paul claims that from tanker to bottle he can produce this solid, nuanced, complex product in as little as 23 days, and his experiments now are merely detail adjustments—a yeast strain here, a new flavor there. That said, he is happy to share a few of the more monumental hiccups along his early learning curve, including a failure to account for the high pectin content in fresh apple juice. "We ran a filtration when the juice first came in, and it clogged the pad within thirty seconds. So we tried a larger pad. Same thing. After two more, I began to rethink the whole thing, but there I was with thousands of gallons of juice."

I could walk you through the steps, outlining the transformation of apples to ambrosia, but I won't. I pride myself on a certain ability to make dull subjects interesting but this technical silk-purse-out-of sow's-ear even goes over my head.

Instead, I'll talk Paul, the artisan Scotto. The approachable Scotto. The acute Scotto—and although his friends tell me that Whitney is not the first young lady to have been smitten by him over the years, I said 'acute', not 'cute'; I leave it to others to determine that.

He's a popular Lodi bloke, though—for sure. Paul's winery's club membership tops 1400, so many that they had to halt members from bringing friends to a recent tasting, the better to serve those they have. Paul's combination of Italian good looks, burgeoning self-confidence and ease around a growing fan base has made him something of a local rock star.

A week after Valentine's Day, his father and I went to visit him at Sera Fina, the Plymouth winery Paul owns and operates along, merely one of a laundry list of his Scotto Family Cellars and Cider Brothers chores.

During the ride, A2 lathered on some personal history, which will occupy its own chapter, and also some history of Sera Fina Cellars—the bailiwick of this one.

In 2007, Sera Fina began as a gleam in the old man's eye, which was probably a gleam from one too many mid-day wine tastings; A2 was supposed to be home by 5:00 that afternoon so he could take his wife to a concert and became totally lost in the Amador foothills. He began to lose his cool, and A2 does not like to lose his cool—he considers it a sign of weakness. So he began to take down phone numbers of any property he passed with a For Sale sign in front, and later, he made a point to call each one to inquire about financing details. He didn't necessarily intend to buy anything, but the idea of an afternoon wasted did not compute in the Scotto worldview, so he made the most of his FUBAR. Without a follow-up call, the number-taking would have been a waste of time. And not wasting time is the way that A2 rolls—even while directionally challenged.

However, it turned out that one of the properties—the twelfth of twelve on the list as it happened—was an ideal site for a winery. Ideal frontage, perfect exposure, knockout view. A2 had struck gold in Amador County, home of the Kennedy Mine, once the deepest gold mine in the world.

Plymouth, CA, the site's zip code address and known variously throughout the years as Puckerville, Pokerville, and Poker Camp, is also in the middle of Zinfandel country, and love it or hate it, the umbilical cord between nearby Sutter Creek and Sutter's Home White Zinfandel is proof positive.

At the time, Paul Scotto was doing remarkably well selling heavy equipment for Sacramento-based Vermeer, living off commissions that before the economic downturn of 2008 were quite commendable. But, he'd served some hard time in the UC Davis enology program, and he had long dreamed of opening a winery. For the time being, the Vermeer job was too good to quit; at least until the time his customers began to have an increasingly difficult time financing big ticket purchases.

And the gold in them there hills proved to be the gleam in the old man's eye: The site of Sera Fina Cellars.

The ground around here actually *is* sort of gold, but the geology books claim it's "consolidated rhyolitic tuffaceous sediments," which I don't have to Google to assume is not what they make best-selling records out of. There are also bright fields of iron-rich red clay, and others littered with massive boulders that are disconcertingly green. They're made of green basaltic rock, fittingly called greenstone, but Zinfandel—the varietal most associated with the appellation–prefers red granite soil.

Zinfandel was never going to be focus of Sera Fina, and Paul Scotto is as like to vinify it under its Puglian alias Primitivo—the Italian name for the varietal. The theme of Sera Fina, besides subliminal, Big Brother admonishments to "Relax" (on t-shirts, on signs in the tasting room, on web site verbiage; it's the mission statement) is Paul's Italian heritage. *Sera Fina* means 'beautiful evening', his wine club is called *La Famiglia* and he makes Barbera, Pinot Grigio and Malvasia Bianco. Behind the tasting room, there's a sight to warm the heart of the most jaded *goombah*: A bocce court.

This is the sort of tasting room that should add a neon sign beneath "Relax" saying, *"There are only two kinds of people in the world—Italians and people that wish they were Italian."*

Or maybe that's better reserved for Al the Wop's, the strange little tavern in strange little Locke that also occupies its own chapter in this book.

Of course, as a lover of Rhône varietals, Paul's grab bag wine list includes a nice selection of Viognier, Syrah and a dry Rosé made from the classic GSM blend, Grenache, Syrah and Mourvedre, and with all these fantastic vinous innovations, what does Paul bring out for me to taste? More cider. This one is Mango Muscat, the latest in a string of experiments he is running in tandem with California Concentrate; it's a bright and refreshing fruity drink—something you might sneak in the privacy of your own home, not something you'd order in a biker bar like Al the Wop's.

Flavored cider is like flavored anything; a niche reserved for the somewhat faint of heart. It's like bubblegum pop—we may all harbor a secret craving for it, but most of us would not fess up to it in society—polite or otherwise.

Unless it was at the 2016 San Francisco Chronicle Wine Competition Public Tasting. If I had a single encompassing accolade to heap upon Paul and Michael Scotto's line of artisan ciders, it was the public's reaction to their William Tell Hard Cider with Strawberry, winner of their category's Best of Class.

I volunteered to pour at the tasting dressed in my Scotto Family Cellars hat, Scotto Family Cellars t-shirt, Scotto Family Cellars cotton zip-front jacket, looking like a NASCAR driver plugging his sponsors or Roger Daltrey on the cover of '*The Who Sells Out.*' Frankly, I don't feel bound by any sense of journalistic ethics that prevent me from supporting the folks who are putting me up in downtown Lodi; this book is an editorial, not an exposé.

That's why I don't mind sharing my personal reaction to the shiny happy joggers and bikers and roller-bladers gliding along the northern waterfront between Aquatic Park and the Marina Green; buff, tan, thin and model-gorgeous beautiful people enjoying a balmy 70° Saturday afternoon. Everybody here seems to assume that just because I am from the winter-ravaged Midwest, where (as the joke goes) the lauded four seasons are almost winter, winter, still winter and the 4th of July, that I *must* love California in February, where the skies are blue and the temperatures tame.

In fact, there is something profoundly disturbing to me (and my innate sense of up and down) when I see people sunbathing in the middle of winter. It upsets the equilibrium; it's like Australians celebrating Halloween in the spring and Christmas in the summer.

What in the world are all these San Franciscans so happy about—did they forget that everything sucks? As a Detroiter beamed down into the middle of Happy Town, I felt like one of those feral children raised by wolves who becomes somebody's civilizing project. Within a couple of hours I was pining for the jungle and the raw meat of the Motor City.

At least the thousands of people in attendance at the Chronicle tasting had an excuse for their grins and simpers: Artificial stimulants. This is the largest public tasting of the largest competition of American wines in the world and it's held inside what looks like a blimp hangar and patrons paying upwards of a hundred dollars a ticket can sample the best of the six thousand entries from 28 states that competed in this year's competition.

An endless string of booths were set up, where pogues like me—or luminaries like Jim Caudill of Hess Collection—strutted their stuff.

I've poured at these sorts of events in the past and I know the score—after tasting a hundred or so wines, many of which are high-octane, punch-in-the-head reds or tart, bone-dry whites, your palate feels like Rocky Balboa's face looked after 15 rounds with Apollo Creed. So, my little table with its bottles of clean, pure, effervescent apple cider was balm in Gilead, a cool shower after a year-long drought. It was positioned to prosper, poised to prevail. But, as I said, having covered these sorts of events in the past, I can state without equivocation that I have never known an individual product with such mass appeal or that could garner such universal "wows" as Scotto's cider. In five pouring hours, I did not record one single thumb down from anybody, man or woman, hipster or oldster, and this included people who claimed they didn't like hard cider and people who had never heard of the Cider Brothers.

Had it been legal to sell case-loads at the tasting (it wasn't) I have no doubt the Scotto's warehouse would currently be empty.

To me, San Francisco Chronicle Wine Competition is the tallest soapbox from which the Cider Brothers could advertise—not in script but in sips. If I pontificate, therefore, it's from sanguine loft of experience.

And anyway, who needs Al the Wop when you've got Paul the Wop and Guido Gold in Amador County?

4. CALLING THE SCHATZ FROM A THOUSAND FEET

On a scale of one to ten, what's the appropriate trepidation level to admit when the dude who is about to take you up in his Cessna 210 Centurion has trouble figuring out how the A/C in his pickup truck works?

And how does that number skew when the pilot is a wise-ass who is not adverse to making cracks about every potential disaster that might occur, including an apparently serious question about my life insurance being up to date? Which it isn't, by the way.

None of this matters if the pilot is Rodney Schatz who has been flying planes for 34 of his 52 years, recently completing is 1200th flight hour, making me the grateful survivor of 1201. We spent that hour cruising over Lodi and surrounding communities, and the view of this fertile, flowing, fantastic wine region from a thousand feet overhead is aw-inspiring. People who namedrop "Napa" and "Sonoma" without blinking an eye are generally surprised to learn that Lodi—which they may or may not have even heard of—is bigger than both of them combined, and by a huge margin. Lodi currently has over a hundred thousand acres planted to grape vines, and it's expanding all the time. Hard to see where such expansion is possible—one thing that strikes you immediately from the bird's eye view is that nearly every place that can be planted to vineyards is planted to vineyards. You'll see some cattle ranches, where the livestock looks like fruit flies climbing on a fermentation tank; you'll see some bottom land still inundated with flood water and vernal pools which are protected due to something called a fairy shrimp—there's Rancho Seco nuclear power plant, which looks exactly like the place where Homer Simpson punches his time card, except that it has been decommissioned since 1989. There's a 1.5-megawatt solar farm on Jack Tone Road south of Hillside Drive and the Camanche Dam power station is capable of generating 10.7 more—thus, in one photo op, you can see three radically different methods of generating electricity, both old school and new.

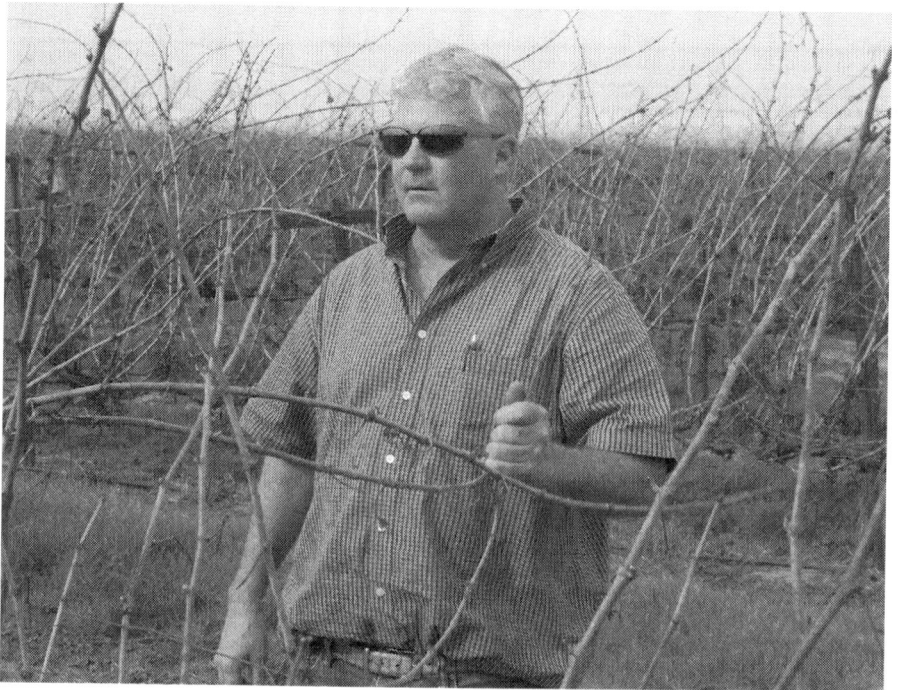

You also see a gaggle of grapes, a volley of vinifera, a zeal of Zinfandel, a covey of Cabernet—of which Lodi produces twice as much as Napa. There a few mom 'n' pop operations remaining, for sure, but most of these are vast, sprawling blocks of corporate-owned or corporate controlled vineyards, some a thousand acres or more. Schatz, formerly the chairman of the California Association of Winegrape Growers, points out the consolidation that has taken place since Constellation bought Robert Mondavi has completely changed the face of wine grape growing throughout the state, and these days, the market for Lodi grapes is pretty much dictated by Gallo and Constellation.

"Every time I had a winery client, Constellation would buy them," he says. "It hurts when you have worked hard to create a product and you can't even sell it to your own wineries at a price where you can survive."

Despite the visual dominance of grape vines from the vantage of a Cessna, California Agricultural Statistics Service insists that San Joaquin County also leads the state in producing apples, asparagus, blueberries, cherries, corn and walnuts. These crops either look like grapes from the sky or they're down there somewhere…

Of the mega-mansions belonging to the county's beautiful people we buzz, at least one does indeed belong to Rodney Schatz. He plays the humble card as we sail overhead, but it's clear that whatever he's getting for his wine grapes from either Constellation or Gallo, it ain't minimum wage.

Which, in California, is now $10 an hour. Before we took to the wild blue yonder, we stopped by one of Rodney's vineyards, and up to his neck in the wild brown yonder—pruned Zinfandel canes in particularly—is Magaro Garcia, an hourly worker who is part of the indispensible flow of Mexican farm hands that form the agricultural foundation of the grape industry, here and everywhere else in California. Unlike a few other growers I have encountered here, Schatz has no problem with the increased wage, and in fact, pays by the vineyard row, so a hard worker has the opportunity to earn considerably more than minimum.

When the time comes, generally late September, these grapes will be harvested entirely at night, the better to pre-chill them and to deliver them to the crush facility cold and first thing in the morning. Rodney Schatz spreads his hands out in an encompassing sweep, envisioning the sight: "This place looks like a Hollywood set at harvest time—huge floodlights, machine harvesters running up and down the rows, taco trucks steaming, loaded and ready for bear."

The shotgun in his pickup truck that I had to move in order to get in may or may not have been loaded, but it isn't bear that Schatz shoots: It's gophers, the bane of local vineyards. There are also owl boxes scattered about, but when I shook one, a big falcon flew out, which is a species just devoutly to be wished. These natural predators earn an excellent living on gopher flesh, and Schatz encourages them with rent free accommodations.

A few vineyards down, also belonging to Schatz, is a block of Teroldego. This is an a red varietal rarely found outside Alto Adige in Northern Italy, and even there it only has a single DOC. There is only about three hundred acres of the grape in the entire state, which is about half the amount of California Centurion, which, beyond the brand of Rodney's single engine plane, I don't know the name.

I'd be willing to bet that there is very little Teroldego grown in the United States, either in or outside California. But somehow, it winds up being Rodney Schatz signature variety, the top-end wine at his winery, Peltier Vineyards. This is the sort of move that may exemplify the huevos of a guy who flies Cessna airplanes—essentially Volkswagens with wings—from Lodi to Boston to sell a few cases of wine. Why? Because most reviews of this intensely-colored, fruit forward wine sound very much like Zinfandel descriptions, and in an appellation where the single most prized and sought-after wine is, in fact, Zinfandel, labeling and trying to sell a bottle of wine that nobody has ever heard of that tastes like Zinfandel, but costs a whole lot more, is the plan of a man with some fortitude.

Safely returned to terra firma, we dove into a bottle of Peltier Vineyards Teroldego 2010, which spend three years in French oak and developed an extremely rich, chocolate and blackberry infused blockbuster that I honestly thought was too young to truly show true colors—the tannins were still gripping at every point across the palate. The wine does show some of the characteristics of old vine Zinfandel, but wraps it up in a package with a bit of spice and mint. It's a luscious mouthful and should hang around for a few more years before it reaches maximum appeal.

I think he's on to something with this grape, no question about it. I dig someone who is willing to take this sort of risk, who has earned his brick in the Lodi wall and who can see the future of the industry—with or without a Cessna Centurion—from overhead.

5. JOHN 'THE GURU' MCCLELLAND: LAST OF THE OLD GUARD

When the guy in the cartoon panel wants to ask the guru about the meaning of life, he has to climb up the side of some mountain in the Himalayas. When I want to ask John McClelland about the meaning of wine, I have to drive up the side of some mountain in Sonoma.

Somewhere in his early eighties, McClelland is uniquely positioned to be my grape guru throughout this Lodi narrative—he joined Almaden when he was in his twenties and didn't move on until he was president of the company. From there, he took over the rudder at Geyser Peak, then Alderbrook, and in a career spanning almost sixty years, he has fraternized and socialized and knocked around with everybody who was anybody in the world's wine pantheon.

In fact, when you show industry folks a picture of him and Robert

Mondavi, they often say, "Who's the guy standing next to John McClelland?"

That may be slightly hyperbolic, but the truth is, McClelland is among the most powerful California wine pioneers left, and the first thing that strikes you about him is how physically powerful he remains. Big as a bear and bald as a billiard ball—he looks a little like Brando in Apocalypse Now—his handshake could crush walnuts, and although he hasn't put a shot since high school, I wouldn't be surprised if he could out-distance nine out of ten athletes at Sonoma Valley High today.

Not that there is anything intimidating about him beyond the sheer magnitude of his memory; the nutcracker handshake is filled with warmth and gentility and the collection of heirloom daggers, blades and combat knives in the glass case over the fireplace is strictly for display.

In a cramped, keepsake-crammed office in a comfortable, but modest hillside bungalow, McClelland immediately whips out is a wine list he wrote for a Hollywood restaurant called Lucey's New Orleans House in 1958. The prices are mind-blowing, the selections museum-worthy and the whole image of a Melrose Avenue clip joint where you went to see and be seen, which served in the day as a who's who of Tinsel Town's glitterati, where you could order a bottle of '53 Lafite Rothschild for $10.50 to wash down a filet mignon priced at $5.00.

"In those days, sommeliers didn't write wine lists, at least in California," John shares. "If you had them at all, they were glorified waiters. The lists were written by people who sold wine, and the reason I was generally more successful at it than the rest was that I never focused on my products. I offered a spectrum of the best wines from around the world, wines from Burgundy, Bordeaux, the Rhine as well as the top California labels at the time."

He adds: "I love to out-geek the geeks."

McClelland's geekery was probably only a small component of his success; he is a persuasive salesman in all aspects of his persona, at once all-knowing and humble, and his reminiscences of the Golden Years in the Golden State could easily fill an afternoon. Throughout his rise through the Almaden ranks, from a Los Angeles sales rep to king of the castle, he encountered a number of dirty rascals. Some of them, like the crew at a winery Almaden bought pouring caramel in a Sherry cask and artificial orange flavoring in the Rhine wine, he set straight. Others, like the Purple Gang's infamous Moe Dalitz who ran the Stardust in Las Vegas, he simply embraced with professional cordiality and sold wine.

In fact, dealing with the Mafia was an occupational hazard if you wanted to sling wine on The Strip in the fifties—beside The Stardust, the Fremont, the Tropicana, the Sands and the Thunderbird were all Our Thing's thing. "You tried to do your job and not make too many mistakes," McClelland laughs.

Among my favorite of his countless industry anecdotes involves Victor Jules Bergeron, founder of the iconic chain of Polynesian-themed restaurants that bore his nickname, Trader Vic. Vic, McClelland suggests, was batshit crazy—but in a good way—and one night Vic called, screaming into the phone that he'd just read a book on 'pyramid power' and wanted all of his wine to be warehoused under makeshift pyramids going forward.

"He was a mad genius," McClelland remembers, "and with nineteen restaurants, a huge customer. So, we built him his pyramid, stored his wines underneath it, and by God, if they did not get better after a few months. I can't explain it."

He can, however, explain the razzle-dazzle rise in the popularity of California Chardonnay, which until the 1960s was something of an afterthought varietal in California, often mislabeled "Pinot Chardonnay." Its questionable value to the fine wine market was due in part, ironically, to its malleability. Chardonnay thrives in a variety of environments, yielding a reasonable crop in many different soil types and climates, but generally produces a flabby, somewhat neutral wine outside a few pockets along the cool, foggy Pacific coast. Prior to Prohibition, it was not a varietal recommended by University of California researchers, and the few acres that were planted to Chardonnay were torn out with the Volstead Act because it was too thin-skinned to make it ship-worthy to home winemakers in other parts of the country.

Following the repeal of Prohibition the only commercial Chardonnay plantings left were at Wente and Masson.

Although in the 1950's UC viticulturists began to recognize Chardonnay's potential in cooler zones like Winkler Region 1, where it could produce lighter, crisper wines with higher acidity, the grape was susceptible to damage from early spring frosts in those regions, and a plethora of viruses in others. By 1960, there were only about 150 acres of Chardonnay in the entire state, mainly in Alameda and Napa counties. Today there are over a hundred thousand acres of Chardonnay, making it the most widely planted wine grape in the state; four times as much is grown than its nearest white competitor, French Colombard.

So what happened? John McClelland points to that fleeting radar blip among wine fads called Pouilly-Fuissé—the Mâconnais meteor-with-a-bullet that hit the American market in the 1970s, just as we were beginning to sniff out affordable, borderline-unpronounceable French wines with which we could show off. You had to learn how to say it, and if you screwed it up, you were instantly branded a wine rube.

Anthony Scotto III with John McClelland

Then, suddenly, the Pouilly-Fuissé marketing juggernaut hit a snag: There wasn't enough of it to go around. Prices began to skyrocket and Americans who were smart enough to pronounce Pouilly-Fuissé proved that they were also smart enough not to get ripped off by Pouilly-Fuissé, which—let's be honest—is a nice, but generally forgettable table wine.

"And then the light bulb over somebody's head switched on," McClelland says. "We realized that we were growing better stuff right here in California. The Paris Wine Tasting of 1976, also known as "The Judgment of Paris," proved it beyond any doubt, and everyone woke up to the quality of California Chardonnay. Far from merely beating out Pouilly-Fuissé, Chateau Montelena from Napa beat a Batard-Montrachet and Puligny-Montrachet."

In the immediate aftermath of these twin vinicultural godsends, California Chardonnay plantings quadrupled, going from 2700 to

11,000 acres in five years, quadrupling again to 45,000 acres by 1988, when it overtook overtake France's total Chardonnay acreage.

In certain ways, the Grasshopper had become the guru.

So, back to the real guru here—John McClelland. At an age when most retired executives would be putting up their feet and counting their Damascus Daggers, McClelland hasn't slowed down much. Some health concerns notwithstanding, his name finally adorns a wine label—better late than never.

J. McClelland Wines is a joint venture between John, Anthony Scotto III and winemakers Paul Scotto, Mitch Cosentino and Mark Smith. Produced by Steele Canyon Cellars of Napa, the brand features a Chardonnay, a Merlot and a Cabernet Sauvignon from the Oak Knoll District and a somewhat fascinating varietal called Charbono—no relation to Sonny—from Calistoga. I say fascinating because, although this particular version is beautifully rich and layered, the grape has had a strange and convoluted history: It's been nicknamed "The Rodney Dangerfield of Grapes" and has probably won more awards under the wrong name than under the right one. Over the years, Charbono has been mistaken for Barbera, Dolcetto and in the Veneto, it was thought to be another varietal altogether, Turca. In Argentina, the grape is called Bonarda, and even then it has no genetic link to true Bonarda, Bonarda Piemontese.

If you are the sort of person who puts stock in such accolades, J. McClelland Charbono has landed scores in the 90s from a number of prestigious publications, including Wine Enthusiast. So did J. McClelland Cabernet Sauvignon. In fact, they've all crested that milestone in one vintage or another.

And thus, I'm obligated to conclude with the fact that the last time an Almaden wine made any serious point-scoring waves among the vignoscenti, John McClelland was probably at the helm. How gratifying it is to see an old and venerable warhorse donning the armor a final time and venturing out into the battlefield to win not only the battle, but the war.

6. MITCH COSENTINO: IT RHYMES WITH 'HERITAGE'

I've always had a love/hate relationship with journalism. I enjoy cutting edge, investigative reporting wherein we dig up Delphinium beds to look for corpses, peek in closets to see if there are any skeletons and hack computers to see if there is any squirrely internet searches that become our smoking guns.

I'm less enamored with the obligations inherent in an interview, wherein I must respect the interviewee's request that I keep some things off the record. What I experience is akin to what in horse racing as chomping-a-the-bit and among crude college frat types as "blue balls."

The bit of information that Mitch Cosentino asked me to keep under my hat has nothing to do with skeletons or Delphiniums or horse racing; it had to do with that all-American Bordeaux blend known as Meritage.

Bordeaux blends used to be called Bordeaux blends until the oddly named U.S. Bureau of Alcohol, Tobacco, Firearms, and Explosives lay a minefield of regulations that effectively emasculated a lot of old school traditions in the American wine industry. Wines that list a specific varietal on the label, like Merlot or Cabernet Sauvignon must contain at least 75% of that grape, which is fine. But Bordeaux blends are by their nature a combination of Merlot and Cabernet (along with a small grocery list of other allowable grapes), but the label cannot legally call it what it is—an emulated Bordeaux. According to the law, this would infringe on the Bordeaux's protected designation of origin. The name "Champagne" works like this too, unless your name is Korbel, Cook's or André and you were grandfathered in.

Mitch Cosentino had no such C.Y.A. clause with his Bordeaux blends, and in 1988, along with a group of frustrated Napa winemakers, he formed an association and held a contest in order to come up with a proprietary name which would reflect the fact that the wine is a Bordeaux blend but cannot call itself a Bordeaux blend. They waded through over six thousand entries, and finally settled on Meritage, a morpheme blend of "merit" and "heritage" and rhyming with the latter. If you insist on Frankifying it to make it sound like "garage"—and many, many wine people do—you sound like a bit of a dope.

Which is one of the reasons, among several others, that I never cozied up to the word, maybe less so when I learned that after all that, in order to call yourself "Meritage" you have to pay the Meritage Alliance a buck for every case you sell, up to $500 per vintage. If you don't, I assume they get their lawyers involved. Now, call me silly, but if you are going to get sued anyway, wouldn't it be easier on your average Dick and Jane "How Do You Pronounce Meritage" Wine Consumer if you simply called your wine "Bordeaux Blend" to begin with and let the legal chips fall where they may? What not eliminate the middleman?

Nonetheless, Cosentino produced "Poet," America's first designated and licensed Meritage.

The blue balls of journalistic integrity were set to aching when I asked Mitch Cosentino what name—out of the six thousand entries—came in second to Meritage. And he told me. And I loved it. And I thought it was a million times better than the one that came in first. But there is, apparently, some non-disclosure agreement Cosentino signed that prevents him from revealing the other names, for reasons that probably make as much sense as paying a buck a case to name your wine something that people neither understand nor can pronounce.

Mitch let the first runner-up name slip in a moment of weakness, and I, as your faithful narrator, will respect his wish and keep that slip-of-the-tongue to myself.

Anyway, it would be silly to suggest that the Meritage controversy—mostly invented by me simply because I get a kick out if it—is a sum-total of Mitch Cosentino's contribution to the Lodi wine scene. Meritage is an important Cosentino subplot, of course, but ultimately a mere radar blip on his very large screen.

One of Napa's most respected winemakers, Mitch Cosentino kicked off his career in Modesto in 1980, when he began producing small lots of custom blends in a corner of a warehouse. The son of a Modesto clothier, he still carries himself with a certain air of sartorial elegance, even dressed in jeans. He's trim and wiry and endlessly animate; his hair is graying and his face shows signs of having spend many decades beneath the California sun, but he still blushes when you kid him about some mystery date he has for Valentine's Day. It's the sort of endearing quality that underscores his talent, making him the sort of winemaker you love to sit and drink wine with.

Cosentino's history of drinking with the Scotto family began in 1986, when A2 and he met at a winery in Escalon. They had the common ground of heritage and handicraft, both being winemaking Italians, and are both A-type personalities, so naturally, they had to end up as sworn enemies or bosom buddies. Fortunately, they took the latter route.

Between 1986 and 2014, before the Scotto family began an actual wine collaboration with Mitch on Steele Canyon Cellars, Cosentino had climbed a tall celebrity vine in Napa. Accolades include being crowned Winemaker of the Year in 2003 and as winemaker for his Cosentino Winery, producing the "Best American Cabernet Sauvignon" in 1986 and "Best Wine in California" in 2002. He can list over a thousand awards he's won and in 35 years, has created, designed, and built 9 wineries in Napa Valley and Lodi.

In short, when Steele Canyon needed a consultant, Mitch offered the complete package: Skill, family history, a big name and a lot of connections. Complimenting the winemaking skills of Paul Scotto and Mark Smith, Cosentino brings long-time relationships with area growers to the table along with a war-chest full of medals.

The trio produces big quality, small lot Napa wines at a reasonable rate, which today is a lot harder to do today than it was 35 years ago when Cosentino learned his winemaking chops. pureCru is his latest label; high end stuff, at prices appropriate to quality.

"I'm what's referred to as a self-taught winemaker," he smiles. "No degree from Davis, although I have lectured about wine at plenty of colleges and universities over the years, including Davis. I produced my first vintages it in a metal building without insulation, relying on swamp coolers for refrigeration, without hot water or floor drains. And do you know what? Most of those wines are still alive today."

I'd be hard-pressed to pigeonhole Mitch Cosentino in a single word, so were I to try, I'd have to invent one. In fact, I'd have to blend two together. Merit and heritage would certainly apply, and I'd let you pronounce it any way you want, but Meritage is taken. So is Hermitage. Heritit? Naw. How about a blend of gumptious and elegant? 'Gumpgant'. I like it. Say it out loud; let it roll off your tongue and repeat it slowly:

"Mitch Cosentino is bumpgant."

Now send me a dollar.

7: LIFE IN THE TALL LAYNE: m2 WINES

My buddy Amy Corron Power thinks Layne Montgomery rules your face off, and I can see why: Like her, he speaks his mind with the sort of mountain burr that makes you think of up-from-the-bootstraps Southern folk who, at the close of the day, would rather let the product do the grandstanding, not the public persona.

In Amy's case, it is the well-written wine column 'Wine Wonkette' and in Layne's, it's the well-made wines at m2 Cellars.

Layne's story, which he tells with just a tad of good ol' boy shucks 'n' gawrsh self-effacement, is really quite compelling: He grew up in a religious household where alcohol was verboten, and to this day, his sister condemns him for making the Devil's Juice for a living. Remember that old joke about Southern Baptists, and the fact that they don't have sex because it might lead to dancing? Layne Montgomery is living proof that they do it anyway.

"My daddy don't dance and my momma don't rock and roll," he snickers, shaking his head at the absurdity of the whole situation: "I didn't take my first drink of wine until I was a junior in college, and then it was—of all things—a Pink Catawba. I knew nothing about wine except the hype, but I instantly knew that the hype couldn't be about Pink Catawba."

Layne is a tall fellow, and everything about his spare, wide-open m2 tasting room is super-sized—twenty foot ceiling, twelve foot door, ten foot 'm2' sign behind the bar, which would be tall if you stood it on end, but granted, that would diminish its efficiency. He wound up here in the Land of the Giants through a labyrinthine path that began with that sip of Pink Catawba, took him through broadcasting school in Arkansas, an ABC job in Little Rock and an operations gig in Grand Junction, where he discovered a different kind of wine game going on at Colorado Cellars. Not that CC was any great massive and venerable icon at the time. Although it bills itself as "the oldest, largest and most award-winning winery in Colorado," I had to double check the next line to make sure it wasn't a typo: "Founded in 1978."

Lodi—where vineyards were already old in 1878—was not yet on Layne Montgomery's radar, but a big, extracted Lemberger made by Colorado Cellars was, and this gave him an idea of the sort of wines that could leave an impression on the soul and not on the molars. For Layne and wine, it was bye, bye Pink Catawba and hello, world.

He took a wine appreciation course and showed up in Napa during the crush of 1984 to learn the basics. That included, in his words, "What a good wine is supposed to taste like."

But when his wife's job took them to Sacramento in the late 1990s and she suggested that he get into winemaking, she meant hobby-level—carboys and five-gallon buckets.

There have been times when he (and maybe she) wishes he'd kept it that way: "I blew the first batch completely, adding too much acid when I shouldn't have; I should have been reducing it—math was never my strong point. Thirty gallons of Cabernet Sauvignon. That wine is not only still around, it's still in its infancy."

Fortunately, Layne quickly mastered the inverse relationship between acid and pH, at least as demonstrated by his 2014 Viognier: It's a beautiful wine called 'Fair Play', using fruit from grown at a 2300 ft. Since Lodi's highest point of elevation is less than fifty feet, Fair Play was clearly sourced from elsewhere—in fact, Eldorado County, just north of Sacramento. It's brisk and balanced, showing lemon pudding notes and a touch of coconut.

The winery incorporated in 2004, and his original partner (the second 'm' in the name; 'Montgomery' is first) bailed while a number of other investors came on board. Too many? That's open to debate, but the entire operation is, according to Layne, a happy blend of "luck, incest and synergy"—at least for the most part. He's barely breaking even, but the wines are showing an uptick in popularity, both locally and abroad. Although production is less than 5000 cases a year, m2 Wines can be found from Alaska to Hong Kong, although—granted—not too many places in between. m2 is largely a Lodi phenomenon, but it is one of those quirky, small-batch envelope-pushers that is painting the face of innovation on Lodi's staid reputation as a production workhorse appellation.

Plus, Layne got a wealth of good stories and he shares them with the folksy ease of a country boy from Springfield, Missouri, which is what he is. On a personal note, I loved that he turned out to be a close friends with an obscure Croatian-Californian winemaker named Milan Vujnic, who is also an obscure friend of mine and who I believe is the only dude in California to make an obscure wine entirely from the Norton grape, a guilty pleasure of mine. On a similar vein, I mentioned that the world's shortest list is composed of Lodi winemakers who import Napa grapes, and it turns out that Lodi's tallest winemaker crowns the world's shortest list: In 2003, a chance comment at a social gathering, in which he said he'd love to buy some Cabernet grapes from Sequoia Grove, passed by word of mouth to gruff old Jim Allen, who immediately arranged to ship him half a ton at the bargain rate of a buck a pound.

Having left the acid reflux disaster in the past, Layne has learned to dial in Lodi's vinicultural details, claiming that working with Old Vine Zinfandel in Lodi is a lot tougher than most people imagine. It took him five years to fine-tune it, especially since (he has found) a lot of it is over-cropped, over-watered and over-fertilized. Winnowing the superstars from the celestial chaff is the first order of duty for any Lodi winemaker intending to excel in the Zin game, and like many Zinophiles who have come before and since him, he names the Soucie Vineyard as among the best.

Meanwhile, the soaring, industrial-chic m2 tasting room with the roll-up door is the culmination of what Layne calls "naïve stubbornness and the grace of God"—who, it turns out, doesn't have such an aversion to hard drink after all.

Finding a more striking surround or a more convivial host? Now, that's a tall order.

8: MIKE MCCAY IS THE REAL MCCOY

Mike McCay is on a treasure hunt to rival the most passionate pirate's, the most corybantic Conquistador's, the most frenzied '49er's. For a Mike strike, where the gold is closer to scarlet-purple, he doesn't need to cross any bounding mains or monstrous mountains, but in order to track it down, he does have to wade through a pretty wide expanse of Lodi grape juice.

At the end of every one of McCay's rainbows there's a pot filled with something he can transform into enological gold: Grapes from small, isolated vineyards scattered throughout Lodi wine country, occasionally neglected, but more often producing fine juice that gets lost amid the production sea that major players like Gallo and Constellation suck up annually. Frequently, this ignoble fate has been the result of land passing through families, where generations of patriarchs were content to have a regular, reliable customer for the produce every year.

These days, some of the sons and daughters have recognized that there might be a better market in small-lot productions and labels that sell for more than a fistful of dollars at Big Box outlets.

According to Mike McCay, who has already identified many of them, there are untold others out there, furtively flourishing, surreptitiously setting, privately producing superb wine grapes, often right beneath the noses of the most observant geek from the Lodi Native project. Mike McCay is a cornerstone of that group, which is dedicated to the proposition that all vineyards are not created equal, and I'll refer to it again shortly.

I'm not sure I've ever been in a wine region where there is such a dramatic fault line between the viticultural generations, but that's probably because I've never before been in a wine region quite like Lodi. It's the bread basket of California wine, producing a quarter of all the wine grapes in the state, but it also has a remarkably quality-friendly climate, with the sort of diurnal temperature shifts required to produce fully ripened grapes while safeguarding vital acidity. As such, the old guard growers had one commercial mindset while their spawn, in many cases, has another.

The American wine revolution (where our wines began to compete on the global stage) straddled that generational shift like the Colossus of Rhodes; one foot in the old world and the other in the new.

McCay is a pretty rugged example of the new.

He dragged himself out of a sick bed to hook up with me inside his tasting room, which happens to be about as unlovely a location, at least from the outside—inside a warehouse backed up in an industrial park off E. Turner—as you could imagine. But the sort of expansive-yet-cozy interior they've eked out here, staffed by bright, pretty young women and ringed with nominally decent artwork for sale, saves the day. Toss in the spectacular range of wines produced in barrel quantities and relying exclusively on native yeasts while focusing on the trueness of winemaking, and you've got a home-run like the one that broke the Louisville Slugger that McCay—a lifelong Giants fan—displays above the juice cooler.

I met a few winemakers in Lodi whose life's goal was to make wine, but I met a whole lot more whose primal mission wasn't. McCay is in the second category—he studied Marine Biology in UC Santa Barbara and soon decided that as far as primal missions go, taking plankton samples inside a mini-sub at midnight didn't have much to recommend it. So he bought ten acres of Lodi land in 1994, farmed it to wine grapes successfully (farming something unsuccessfully in Lodi is something you have to work at) and began to vinify a personal stash in old milk vats. He also had a chemistry background, which helped him come to terms with the treasure trove of vineyard sites throughout the region.

"I make wine in a style that I like, not necessarily to flood the market," he says. "If I do it that way, I can maintain the passion for my product. It's a lot easier to sell stuff you like."

"Look around," he continues, indicating the somewhat primitive ambience. "I don't court throngs of visitors; people come here to seek them out. I don't need sales reps—restaurants call me."

No brag, ma'am—just fact. McCay Cellars wines can be found in some of the trendiest restaurants in California, like Quince in San Francisco, Biba's in Sacramento and Nobu in Malibu. These tend to be sommelier-friendly wines; wines that are clean and bracing, an honest exposé of the fruit. His batch sizes are miniscule—he produces about 4,500 cases annually, but 20 to 25 different wines. His reds are intense—big without being muscular, assertive without being aggressive, opulent without being gilded.

But the whites were the real show-stoppers for me, because—silly boy—I didn't yet realize that the Lodi terroir is so superbly suited for producing layered, silken, spicy whites that when the French delegations come to town, they're shocked that Lodi does not produce more of them.

Vinter/growers like Mike McCay are trying to edge the needle over. For him, there are two periods during each vintage that he rates as monumentally more important than any of the others: The January prune and véraison, when he begins to drop fruit to determine ultimate yields per vine.

"If that's not handled correctly, problems turn up later that the winery can't fix. When I buy grapes from other vineyards, I try to bring the growers over to my side early, even when they think I'm nuts, being wasteful. I tell them I'll pay them for eight tons an acre, then make them drop fruit during the season so that they only produce three. But that's key. Do a good job in the vineyard, and the wines will take care of themselves."

I could (and do) rave about his exotically tropical and floral Viognier, but I stop the presses over his Muscat, 2013. It's rare to see anyone outside the Grands Crus of Alsace attempt—let alone nail—a dry style of this sometimes overly-perfumed varietal. Here, the aromatics are anchored, reined by elegance and a striking herbal nose, with woodruff and lavender hovering above oregano and ginger. The tones are subtle but luscious, with honey and lychee and the somewhat passé descriptor muskiness, actually sort of a perfumed and earthy spice and a hallmark of the grape.

This emerged as my personal favorite of the whites, but the reds are a toss-up of superlatives. All are deliberately extracted to the point that you take notice, but not to the point where you're knocked down. Cinsaut, Carignane, Petite Sirah, all from vines that range in age from thirty years old to over a hundred.

But, true to the heritage grape of Lodi, it is in crafting Zinfandel that Mike McCay sends his enological feelers out across the appellation, currently producing six vineyard-designated Zins with three more coming next year. And, in the future, I imagine that he'll bottle as many labels as unique terroirs his perpetual-motion treasure hunt turns up.

Naming a vineyard on a bottle of American wine is a tradition that post-dates most of these plantings; Heitz Martha's Vineyard Cabernet Sauvignon was the first, and that didn't happen until 1966. As a marketing hook, it has probably been somewhat abused, since the cachet that a winery is aiming for is the suggestion that a named vineyard is a better vineyard, and that's not always the case.

In the Lodi Native Project's case, you can be pretty sure that it is. These innovative cheerleaders have taken solemn vows on the souls of their progeny to adhere to sensible viticulture and minimalist winemaking techniques, especially, using native yeasts exclusively, oak sparingly and filtering/fining not at all. It's a Zinfandel project, but ironically, the focus of the wine, from six growers who are part of the collective, is not on the flavor of the varietal but the flavor of the vineyard. Five of the growers are in the Mokelumne River sub-appellation, and one is in Clement Hills.

The press for the Project has been phenomenal, probably because the group's mission statement includes us little old wine writers: "To demonstrate to more sophisticated consumers, media (print and blogosphere..." and don't we just sit up and take notice when somebody in the winery sits up and takes notice?(!)

Not much to notice at the McCay tasting room beside the lovely lass with the pour spout and the array of pure, terroir-driven wines that raise the bar for the whole Lodi wine game. The setting may put the "industrial" back in "chic," but as far as a treasure hunt, I see no reason to look farther.

Let's drink and leave Mike to do the heavy lifting.

9: A3'S NOT YELLING—HE'S EXCITED

Trying to condense the whirling dervish life-force that is Anthony Scotto III into a single day? That's a job for a word distillery with more plates than my meager talents command, but try I shall: I followed him from dawn to dusk over what he claimed was a 'typical' workday.

Yet, watching him dart through his rounds quickly turned out to be like watching a film on fast-forward, only without a rewind button. Recording details was futile and merely keeping up became the goal. If you want to give it a shot yourself, my best advice is, "hang on for dear life and wade through the impressions later."

A task at which I am currently engaged.

A3's large circle of friends and relatives seem to agree on one point: Hyperkinesias has pursued A3 since childhood, as a plague or as a gift, depending on who you ask. He seems to shrug it off; to him, it's neither

63

a boon nor a curse, but merely the kai that animates him—a congenital blowtorch to the back of his head. But this is not a question worth pursuing as it becomes equally clear that his business mantra (like his father's) is not built around ego or personal accomplishments, but rather is founded upon the notion that success depends primarily on hiring people who are better at doing things than you are.

As he relates it, A3's story floats on a sea of mentors, and sometimes you need to remind yourself that today's sprawling state of Scotto, encompassing nearly four-dozen brands, though not entirely his handiwork, began at his instigation—even, perhaps, at his insistence.

This success is today multifaceted and manifold, but at the root of it appears to be a gentle technique that A3 refers to as "the art of listening."

"Those who ignore history are doomed to repeat it," he reminds me, referencing some monumental failure or other (not his), and coming from most people, it would sound unstoppably cornball. But Anthony receives a dispensation from San Diego State University—his degree in History and upon graduation, he had his mind set on becoming a teacher. He pursued the requisite certification and put in some substitute teaching hours, an experience he claims taught him the rudiments of addressing a clever crowd while coming across as concise, believable and honest. "A frikkin' awesome experience" is how he describes the government classes he taught, lending groundwork to the way he approaches clients and employees today.

"I learned discipline, lesson planning and how to act under steady state of pressure," he says. "They certainly taught me how to focus drive."

Key to that drive—a driving, decisive need to avoid ignoring history, remains one of A3's core competencies, and in the many hours I spend with him, the memory that pops up most frequently involves him as a child sitting around the family table during Sunday dinners—which, he admits, often devolved into shouting matches—and taking his private solace in listening to his grandfather (A1, Anthony Sr.) spinning tales of Scotto genealogy, the wine business, the Roman empire and the world at large.

"I began to see our role as caretakers of a greater program. We're part of a flow, and we each have our own contributions. If history teaches us anything, it's that there are very few people whose input into the whole can be removed without bringing down the house of cards."

Indeed, it true: I'm touched that he's touched by such touchstones; it reveals two facets of his character that seem to carry through his frenetic approach to life. First, a high regard for his elders, and second—and perhaps more importantly—an ability, even a need, to find value in everyone. A1, who died in 2013, receives some occasionally mixed press, even within his own own family ("He was a good father, but a lousy leader" is how A2 sizes him up), but A3 has instant recall about the plus side and is willing to minimize the rest. This is a quality that surfaces repeatedly in the Scotto's attitude toward those who work for them, and the stories of bailing out (legally, financially and emotionally) employees after bouts with the law, with personal implosions, with drugs, are legion. This is the land of the second chance; the Kingdom of Benefit of the Doubt. Naturally, no names, but most of the folks in whom the Scottos showed faith went on to be productive, energetic employees whose current loyalty is the stuff about which bosses dream.

These behind the scenes acts of Samaritanism may, in fact, be the physical embodiment of the Scotto mantra, where everything balances on behaving like a Scotto, or, as they say, "Who we are..."

I noticed quickly that everyone who was a beneficiary of this mantra all had one thing in common—they could do things that Anthony, his brothers, his sisters, his father, could not, and so they were retained to become part of the pyroclastic family flow. To isolate the particular lava chunk that A3 clambered aboard, we have to return to yesteryear—2000, in particular, the day when he graduated college. That is a significant day in the life of any Scotto kid from this generation, because that is the day that Anthony Scotto II pretty much turns the financial obligations of survival over to the child in question.

"His last official, obligatory act as father: He bought me a suit, five shirts, five ties and a pair of wing-tips. That got me through a number of interviews, a few early job offers with some major companies; entry level, of course."

But the leap from the diving board into the family work pool did not happen that year, or the year after that. A3 tried to settle into an industry job—he was thinking big from the outset and made it through to the final cut at Gallo and opted for Coors, but his heart never really was in it. His father—then comfortably ensconced within the fine little bailiwick he'd carved out as caretaker of the Villa Armando brand and not looking for a partner—offered him a strange bit of advice; advice which in retrospect, was genius:

"He told me to write a manual for my replacement. Codify the methods, the "whys" behind everything the job entails. It allowed me to understand the mechanics of what I was doing, and as a result, visualize instantly the number of changes I could think of to do it better."

He honed those mechanics over the next few years, and following the earnest exchange along Embarcadero mentioned earlier in this book— the man-to-man heart-to-heart in which he and his father came to an understanding that Anthony III had a role to play in bringing the family business into a new century—he understood that there was a huge market open to a company capable of producing big quantities of quality wine and an affordable rate. And that comfortable bailiwicks were fine, but one should at least consider that there was a whole kingdom out there, ripe for the picking.

And A2 considered it. As history indicates, he ultimately did more than warm to the idea—he leaped at it.

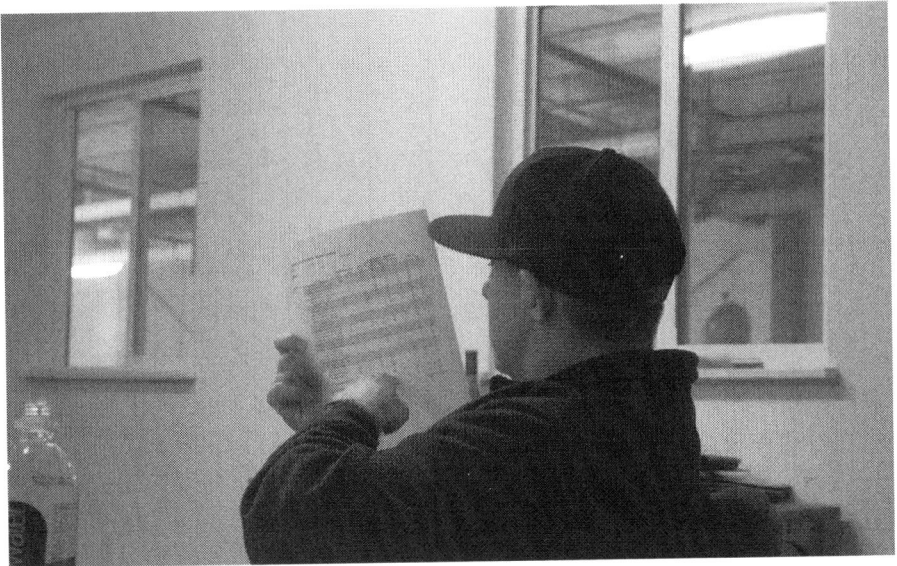

First, his eldest son embarked on a series of educational missions that culminated in what can be viewed as the story of The Three Mentor-teers, with A3 playing the pivotal role as d'Artagnan. He spent time with some older dudes in New York, men he claimed had old dude mentalities—not necessarily a negative; after that, he did a week in Chicago trying to figure out how wine brokering works. But it was back in California wine country that he found his most formidable allies, his Athos, Porthos and Aramis, and this coalesced into the triumph rate that allowed him to weld together a viable business plan.

Two of these figures have their own chapters here; first, the Athos of the equation, the elder statesman, still energetic despite his years, former CEO of Franzia who has forgotten more industry scuttlebutt than most people ever knew, John McClelland. McClelland taught A3 the gentlemanly side of sales—which was not to say he wasn't tough as a teacher, as counsel or as a partner in the Scotto's tribute 'John McClelland' series. It means that, despite a physical stature which remains imposing despite his eighty-plus years, he understood that the wheelings and dealings in the trade can be done with class and dignity while maintaining both ethics and a bottom line.

The tale's Porthos is clearly played by Mitch Cosentino—Dumas describes him as the group's extrovert, a lover of wine, women and song. Cosentino is all that and a technical whiz to boot; he works alongside Paul Scotto in crafting the Steele Canyon label—top shelf wines from Napa. Mitch is multi-generational mentor, having first met A2 in 1986 when the Cosentino Winery was about to make serious waves in Napa; that was also the year his "Poet" blend became America's first designated and licensed Meritage. Cosentino went on to win awards as "Winemaker of the Year" (2003) and "Best Wine in California" (2002), all of which made him a recommendable partner. But don't downplay the Italian connection—those roots run deeply through much of what the Scotto family does, and I noticed a distinct tendency to surround themselves of men and women who share a heritage, often translated into a binary view that suggests that the world is composed of Italians and everybody else.

Bob Walker is not Italian, and he's not Aramis either—but Aramis is the only Musketeer left. Aramis was depicted as unstoppably arrogant, and that, perhaps, is the polar opposite of Bob's character. A3 may have learned the philosophy of sales from John McClelland, but Walker is, as

A3 puts it, "all about the nuts and bolts of salesmanship; the block and tackle."

As Marketing Manager of Scotto Cellars and the J. Woods Beverage Group, Walker is in equal parts squeakily cautious and Aramis-bold in his business strategies, and I must say, when it came to this book, he took me aside and asked me politely to avoid some of the saltier conversations I'd had with the Scotto clan lest it show them in a somehow tarnished shade of gold. But I see no reason for that, of course—a few personal stories aside, the Scottos can lay claim to being honorable men. Not only that, they are are loyal to the overriding code of friendship to which Walker also subscribes: Unus pro omnibus, omnes pro uno.

Armed with this trio of backup brains, A3 has, since 2004, built the family brand into force that is reckoned with all across the wine world, with tendrils extending into countless crevices and niches, with more being evaluated every day. Under his CEO-hood, Scotto's jitterbug confidence and kudo-spreading style has grown the company to encompass an international market and relationships in every state. He went from zero to two hundred distributors in under two years, primarily piggy-backing a strategy of providing the sort of quality, inexpensive California blends that the independent contractors had no access to; blends, he'll tell you, is the base of the business: "The biggest distributors didn't buy into the concept at first, but the smaller ones did. We offered them an alternative to listing primarily low-cost imported wines."

A3's father is quick to point out that the growth trajectory of the family-run company is his son's success. Although A3 owns the LLC, Villa Armando remains an anchor brand Scotto Family Cellars and Villa Armando remains in A2's bailiwick—part of a Scotto wine legacy that has tracked them several generations. A2 remains the caretaker of the company's heart and soul as well as the lifeblood still sold in jugs, the heirloom elixir that Anthony Sr. used to peddle door to door in New York.

The Scotto outreach has now expanded to include a new generation, three of whom are Anthony 3 and his wife Alyssa's. It is the intention of all concerned that these three, at least, will not need to corner their father on the Embarcadero to find a berth in the kingdom.

In fact, A3 is a huge sports fan and once dreamed of playing professional baseball; part of his elemental understanding is that any chase—whether it's for a pennant or a sales goal—begins and ends with building the right team. It remains one of his fondest fantasies that his children will be eager to be and the company motto will read 'Six Generations of Good Taste.'

10: CONCENTRATE, COGITATE AND CULTIVATE: THE ALEXANDERS AND THE REINCARNATION OF PYTHAGORAS

Dennis Alexander is not only highly mathematical and highly Greek, he is the physical reincarnation of the great Ionian philosopher Pythagoras.

This is not my assessment; I'm not much for Euclidean geometry, and the only thing I remember about Pythagoras beside a2 + b2 = c2 is a quote describing the relationship of patterns in nature, whether inanimate or lyrical: "A stone is frozen music."

"The reincarnation of Pythagoras" is Dennis Alexander's personal self-assessment—and he is a man of such mystery and depth that it's hard to find reason to argue.

It is also hard to hold a conversation at all—Dennis is old enough to have known a couple of Pythagoras' contemporaries and he is suffering

71

from what appears to be a debilitating malady of the mind that causes him to lose track of what he is saying mid-sentence and go blank from time to time.

And do not get me wrong: That's fine since his lucid moments sparkle with such wit and wisdom that the lag times seem irrelevant.

Among a volume of intriguing characters in Lodi, I met this particularly intriguing one over the worst BLT on the planet. I won't say the name of the diner that served it, but I will suggest that when your sandwich has only three ingredients, it should be possible to nail down a minimum of one of them. Fail on a level of epic-ness to rival Odysseus. But the meeting was arranged by Anthony Scotto 2 and his son Anthony Scotto 3, and they sat in on the conversation and revealed a lot about themselves as well: Namely, that if they are themselves reincarnations of anyone, it's Job.

Because, alas, that's the level of patience required to provide Alexander the space to share his story; but it is bestowed upon him with deference and pride. Alexander's life has been filled to the brim with introspection and innovation and as far as the Scottos are concerned, a little incoherence toward the end makes him that much more endearing.

A2 and A3 could have prepared me, but the respect they feel for old Dennis is such that they trusted me to level-set my own expectations and adjust my interview accordingly, no questions asked.

And so I did.

The three of us sat stoically, silently, supportively, and for a long time, too. But, although interviewing Dennis Alexander was my morning's raison d'être, for Scottos it was not. They are busy fellows who generally operate on overdrive—they may have viewed the interlude as downtime, but I don't think so, because I have seen them defer to men who they admire many times, for as long as it takes, offering them whatever time and space required to be the sort of men that the hourglass has dictated that they must be.

Like mathematics in Greece, Dennis Alexander's story runs back through essential Lodi history to nearly the beginning; he started out with a small home-winemaking retail business in the '60s, and, along with his brother George and a couple partners, began importing canned grape concentrate from Spain.

Grape concentrate is exactly what you think it is—pressed juice with some of the water removed, then pasteurized. Grapes are picked, on average, at a sugar level of about 24° Brix—after concentration, it is around 68 ° Brix. Grape concentrate was (and is) a staple in home winemaking kits along with pre-measured portions of yeast, sterilizer, nutrients and everything else you'd need to make a bottle of drinkable wine in your cellar. You didn't wind up with Château Le Snoot, but the system made winemaking mistakes difficult and the end result was the equivalent of a mid-priced grocery store wine, which you could make for about a third the price. I know, because my father was sold on the notion, and always seemed to have a batch of something bubbling away in the cellar.

In retrospect, I bet the kit he used came from Dennis Alexander, because at the time, there weren't many outlets selling them.

As it happened, when Dennis got into the kit business there were no California processors concentrating their own juice, and it didn't take the wisdom of the ancient Greeks to see a fillable niche in the domestic market. It did take something close to genius to look at a huge, commercial Hills Brothers Coffee vaporizer and figure out how to retrofit it for wine grapes.

"I remember that other wineries thought we were nuts," Dennis says. "But we found the inventory space we saved storing concentrate was amazing. Our first concentrate was Ruby Cabernet, an Olmo (Dr. Harold Olmo, UC Davis) variety, a cross between Cabernet Sauvignon and Carignan. It produces an abundant crop in the Central Valley, and the home winemakers loved it."

The Alexanders set up shop in Acampo, in an area known as Crush District 11 on California grape pricing charts, and begin to scour auctions for used industrial appliances—a lot of it rigged by Dennis using dairy equipment—building up the business, adding other grapes, expanding the horizons of the DIY crowd to, and finding a huge market for varietal concentrates at existing wineries.

This outlet—wineries—becomes, perhaps, the most widely-known closely-held secret in the annals of California winemaking—one that is spoken of in hushed tones in the parlor with the same fingers-to-the-side-of-the-nose that the parents of pregnant teenagers once used when they sent little Peggy Sue to live with her aunt in Kankakee for the rest of the school year. The TTB—the governing bureau that oversees wine laws—permits the use of concentrated fruit juice in commercial wine, even allowing wine to be made of nothing except concentrate with no requirement that the label mention it.

Legally, if concentrate is added, it may be added in any quantity, with the only stipulation being that it must be the same variety as the rest of the mix. On the surface, this practice may seem somewhat ho-hum, but consider that in California, chaptalizing wine—adding sugar to increase either sweetness or end-product alcohol, even to levels mandated by law—is illegal. In theory, this prevents winemakers who have grown or purchased tart, substandard grapes from artificially boosting the oomph by adding sugar without adding grape solids. Once an end product has reached legal minimums for alcohol, it can compete commercially for shelf space—that all-important consummation that most wineries devoutly wish. The no-chaptalization standard is, in ways, a hold-out law in a system that currently allows a California winemaker to artificially adjust acid levels, tannin levels, extraction levels and to filter out flaws like VA and over-the-top alcohol.

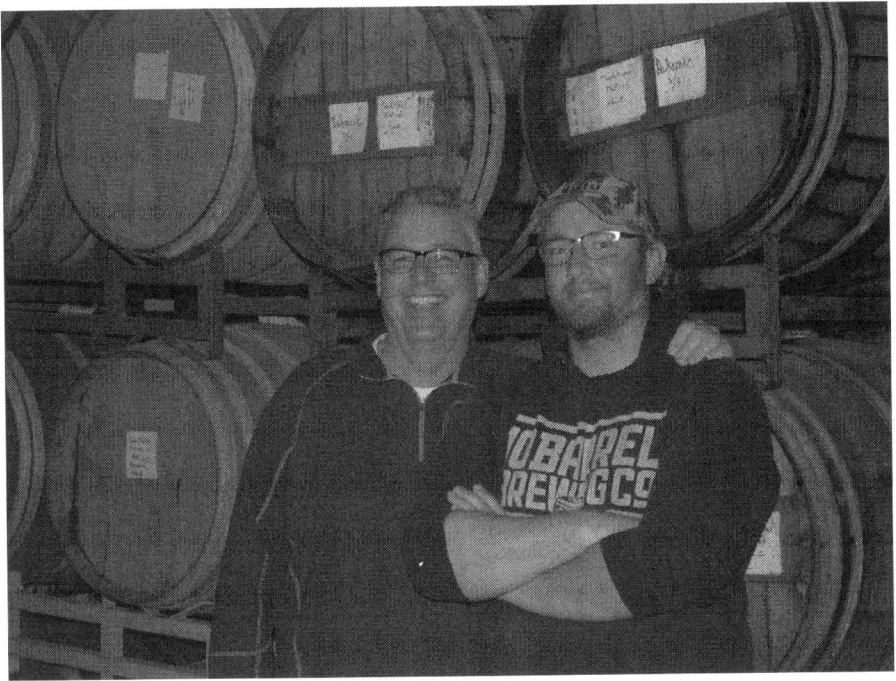

As far as I can determine, the addition of concentrated fruit juice (occasionally from grapes the winemaker him/herself supplies from a bumper vintage and holds until needed) is a logical and wholesome alternative to dumping in character-free sugar, which in the beautiful terroirs of California should not be necessary.

One fairly prominent winemaker who disagrees with me is Adam Lee of Siduri and Novy Family, who told Wine Spectator in 2013 that he has broken the chaptalization laws on more than one occasion. His goal, he maintained, was to increase alcohol in lean years without adding the flavors inherent in concentrated fruit juice. I understand the concept, of course; the danger in excusing Adam when he breaks the law occasionally is that you have less excuse for insisting that his half-assed Cali colleagues, intent on saturating the market with cane sugar wine, follow any TTB regulations ever.

Slippery slopes are one thing, but this one is clogged with granulated sucrose.

And in any case, if a winemaker (and there are a few who do) believes that adding cane sugar to bump up the product is acceptable (even though it's illegal) it's really hard to understand the silly justification for not wanting to legally bump with grape concentrate of the same varietal.

Of course, the fact remains that many—if not most—major winemakers use some grape concentrates in a lot of their wines, not only in California, but in every growing region across country. I'd name some mighty big names if I could without engendering wrath and bad will—not from the wineries, to whom I am not beholden—but from the Alexanders, to whom I am beholden purely on a friendship level.

These clients are their bread-and-butter, and if they don't want the exposé in this edition, I won't do it.

And of course, they don't: Tom Alexander, Dennis's son and the fellow where the dynasty's dynamics now concentrates, told me: "Whenever I show up at a big wine function in Napa or Sonoma, I know everybody's name, but apparently, nobody knows mine…(!)"

I stopped by California Concentrate's nerve center in Acampo, where Tom has his hands on the rudder, the vaporizer and the dozen other contraptions and permutations that the family has put together over the years. The morning I visited, Tom's son was cooking a batch of wort; the Alexanders have also gotten into malt extract for beer making.

"Most canned malt on the market is pretty low grade," Tom assured me. "Mom and Pop beer making shops carry the standard brands, mostly imports. We're trying to raise the bar on what's available."

Not only that, but a massive niche has opened for all-natural extracts from an entire cornucopia of fruits and veggies—the list expands along with the trends. Beside ever-changing 'it' flavors that Americans glam on to, the globe boasts countless regional preferences. Making a beverage entirely from for example, bananas or guavas, is impractical. California Concentrates are produced with pure fruit and pack a lot of focused flavor into a small volume. Organic beverages can use their concentrates and maintain the USDA label, and, as Tom points out, "The world does not grow enough mulberries for all the mulberry drinks on the market, especially in China and Korea. Most of them are simply coconut water with mulberry concentrate added."

And that goes for beverages labeled carrot, watermelon, blueberry, pomegranate, boysenberry, etc. Like the TTB, the FDA has all sorts of regulations regarding juice labeling, and the amount of actual soluble fruit solids that a beverage contains varies by variety, but is usually between a low of 6% for rhubarb and a high of 25% for banana. Frankly, the chart covers a lot of exotic fruits I've never heard of: Youngberry, acerola and guanabana among them.

But I do know muscat and mango, and Paul Scotto, whose family has been customers of California Concentrate for two generations, has put the finishing touches on William Tell Apple Mango Muscat Cider using mango concentrate from California Concentrate. I tried it and it sensuous and lush; mango is one of those fruits that makes itself manifest in subtle, textural ways as well as a sunny sort of gentle sweetness.

When the tech boys start talking about concentrating juice—mango, muscat, carrots or youngberries—the conversation turns to stuff that is Greek to most of us: Cloud stabilization, essence recovery, acid ions, a lot of 'de' things—de-oiling, de-aeration, debittering. Each fruit has its own parameters, so understanding how concentrate is made is a little like understanding how cars are made. Different products have different processes.

In general, Tom points out, fruit for concentrating is handled like fruit for winemaking; it comes in either raw or as juice, and is enzyme-checked and chilled, the sooner the better—it turns out that in this biz, 30°F is your friend. When the reduction begins, the juice passes through a mechanical vacuum vessel to drop the pressure, and this is perhaps the most critical step in making quality concentrate. Water, as we learned in tenth grade physics, boils at 212°F, but with dissolved solids (especially sugars), the boiling point rises. And the hotter the juice, the more the subtle qualities your are trying to enhance are affected, and rarely for the better—a rule of thumb (though not without exception) is that foods that you are accustomed to eating raw will not fare well when exposed to high heat. And that covers most of the 26 fruits and vegetables that California Concentrates processes.

Under a vacuum, the boiling point of juice decreases with the air pressure; this is why water would boil at 160°F on top of Mt. Everest if you were up there and in any condition to try it. For most of Tom Alexander's base juice, 135°F is sufficient to boil off the water while retaining most of the delicate aroma compounds.

By most, of course, Tom means everything except those volatile taste molecules that are lighter than water vapor and have evaporated in the concentration process. This requires a second step—essence recovery. It is essentially a way of distilling the essence-bearing vapors by forcing them through a series of baffles and condensing them, much as the process of making booze from fermented liquid works. The recovered flavors are then reintroduced to the concentrate, giving it additional intensity; additional spirit.

The intensity and spirit that has accompanied the Alexanders through the eons, perhaps since before the Common Era (Pythagoras, 570 BCE – 475 BCE) shows up again in the auxiliary operation, the artisan wine vinegar that they make in an outbuilding far from the main fruit concentrate plant, where the juice might not appreciate the vinegar cultures.

Kimberly Wine Vinegars (Tom Alexander's brand) relies on a French technique—méthode d'Orleans—wherein the transformation of the ethanol in wine to acetic acid via bacteria happens slowly, inside oak barrels. The resulting vinegar is less acidic than commercial white vinegars, terrifically mellow and far more complex that most of the vinegars you've probably tasted. As is the hallmark of Alexander's fruit concentrates, the varietal vinegars retain the subtle characteristic of the mother fruit and/or wine and the terroir in which they were grown.

Meanwhile, back at the diner, over half-eaten BLTs with limp lettuce, soggy tomatoes and rock-hard bacon, Dennis is off in some Ionian taverna, talking mathematics with some folks he met. I am getting the impression that this really happened, and is not some vision from his previous life, and the story, with all its punctuated pauses and detached doldrums, is really quite amazing. His stories unfold in their own way, at their pace, with their own quietude, and to appreciate them, you have to settle in for the long haul and let the wisdom polymerize with the measured evolution of wine vinegar in a balsam barrel.

Which the BLT could certainly have used in place of the viscous slathers of emulsified crap that is commercial mayonnaise. Maybe a spritz of reclaimed bacon essence and a little concentrated lettuce would have helped. Or maybe the whole sub-par sandwich could have been extracted, de-oiled, de-aerated, debittered and added to a bottle of coconut water.

Facetious, of course: But the quality of the raw material is the foundation to Dennis' success and to the reputation of California Concentrate has spent half a century shoring up. Both Aristotle and Ptolemy had paradigms, so it is no wonder that the reincarnation of Pythagoras might see the pure essence of anything to be the sort of project he'd be willing to undertake. After all, in the end, the formula here is simple: Bacon2 + Lettuce2 + Tomato2 = BLT∞.

I have a sense that I may not have another chance to sit down with Dennis Alexander, at least not in this lifetime, but I am gratified to think that there may be other opportunities in the endless cycle that lies just beyond Mt. Olympus.

11. 'ACQUIESCE' MEANS 'ACCEPT WITHOUT PROTEST'

Hi-falutin' British wine journalists know something about wine; I think we can all acquiesce to that observation. Likewise, we accept without protest the statement that Lodi has built a reputation on juicy, boldly flavored Zinfandel and soft, rich Cabernet Sauvignon—in fact, Lodi crushes more of each than Napa and Sonoma combined.

So what does one do when a famous British wine journalist rolls into town and announces that Lodi is better suited for white varietals than for Cabernet Sauvignon?

If you are Sue Tipton, you acquiesce.

Not that she wasn't already well down the acquiescence turnpike before Oz Clarke showed up: Her favorite wine (other than her own) has always been white Châteauneuf-du-Pape and when she began planting vineyards in and around Acquiesce, she wanted to duplicate it—the original incarnation being, in her words, "a bit spendy."

This is the Irish talking; she's a County Cork-American who made it to California after following a meandering path from northwest Chicago to Kalamazoo, Michigan (where Concord vines on her property wound up in Welch's grape jelly). From there, the road less traveled went to Sweden, then to Castlerock, Colorado, then to Dallas, Texas and then to Portland, Oregon where she discovered how exuberant wine at seven dollars a bottle could be. That was in the mid 1990s, when Willamette Pinot Noir was still in search of a place on the global wine stage and as such, was priced to move—that same bottle of wine today would likely sell for four or five times as much.

Ultimately, her husband's job—designing revolutionary, automated warehouses for companies like Coca-Cola—brought them to California, and in 2003, they picked up a piece of property on Tretheway Road in Acampo, just northwest of Lodi. She was initially attracted to the old barn on the site, and then, to the twelve acres of Old Vine Zinfandel—a step up from Concord. But winemaking was not on her "Before I Die" list, at least not on a commercial scale. The Tiptons' plan was to sell the Zinfandel grapes to local wineries, not vinify it, and that's what they do to this day. It wasn't until Sue planted a test plot of Grenache Blanc that did 'exceptionally well' that she began to consider that she might be able produce a white wine in the style of the Châteauneuf blends she loves on acres she already owned; wines that grandstand fruit and herb and flowers and spice in a complex cornucopia of lusciousness.

She planted as many CdP cultivars as as she could find, many from Jason Haas of Paso Robles' Tablas Creek, who is the go-to dude for these kinds of cuttings. And she insists that Oz Clarke's bombastic field trip to Lodi in 2011, during which he pronounced Lodi an ideal climate for the production of white grapes—certainly better than for Bordeaux-

82

style reds—merely confirmed what she already suspected:

In Acquiesce, she had found a little slice of Rhône away from Rhône.

The Clarke pronouncement, outlined in an interview with the local Lodi News-Sentinel (which I quote frequently throughout this book), ran this way:

"In Europe, we get a lot of wine from further south in California, and frankly I don't like that stuff very much. You get south of Stockton and Modesto and you start saying, 'This stuff shouldn't be made into wine.'

It's high-yield, but it has a very low flavor. It's all souped-up, sugared-up pretend wine with a huge marketing budget, and it does California no good whatsoever."

Lodi is different. There is something here. You go 20 or 30 miles south, and you've lost it. But it makes absolute sense. You look at the maps with the Delta and the hills and you see how the wind comes through the Carquenez straight and the first place it gets is here. And then it dissipates; south, north or wherever. But once the wind has been here, it's going to lose its power as it travels on. But you in Lodi have this small area. That's the great thing about wine; small areas matter. Napa and Carneros aren't big."

When grilled about Lodi's limitations, the wizard called Oz continued:

"Lodi has very sandy loams. And loam basically means you can't ripen Bordeaux. You can't ripen Cabernet; you might ripen Merlot. But you should be making rosé and looking at white wines. It's your place. It's a place that should not say, 'We should do what Napa does,' or, 'We should do what Sonoma does.'"

"You need to grow more whites, but I think there is too much Chardonnay here. Everyone else makes Chardonnay. You make good Chardonnay, but Clarksburg makes it better."

It sounds like Oz was preaching to the choir—a choir composed of conductor Sue Tipton and her chorus of Grenache Blanc, Rousanne, Viognier and Picpoul, et al...

And, oh, that Viognier. Mmm, that Picpoul. When I stopped by the tasting room at Acquiesce, it was closed: According to the sign out front, Sue had sold all the wine and there was none left. That's a good sign type of sign. People interested in tasting her wines, not just talking about her wine, will have to wait until mid-March, when the new vintage comes out. But I was fortunate enough to be tagging along with local wine legend Randy Caparoso that day, so I got to line jump.

The tasting room is within the old barn that first attracted Sue and her husband to the property; it used to be the storage area for a walnut farm and there is a filled-in pit in the original concrete that once held walnut shells.

There's a fun chalkboard over the area where we sit—it is titled "Before I Die..." (yeah, Sue's now a commercial winemaker) and it leaves spaces blank for patrons to write down bucket list wishes. On the day I was there, "Golf Pebble Beach" and "High-Five Sammy Hagar" were prominent.

That morning, the headline of the Lodi Sentinel read "Napa Pioneer Peter Mondavi Dies," and since Peter Mondavi was a Lodi grade-schooler before he was a Napa pioneer, I asked Sue if I could write "Meet Peter Mondavi" on her chalkboard, then immediately cross it out. I thought it would make a good intro photo on the chapter I am now—because of his death while I was in town—sort of obligated to write.

Guess who's a good sport?

Guess who's also a world class winemaker? Without a degree from UC Davis or a resumé that includes multiple apprenticeships in established cellars? The woman with the grape jelly vines, that's who—Sue Tipton.

The Acquiesce experience begins on the outside of the bottle, though: It's a svelte Saverglass original called a 'Sabine' and it is designed with feminine flourishes and motile curves—a lot like Sue Tipton. She uses this shape to house all of her wares which are styled like the Saverglass and her: Rich and tactile, floral and feminine; entities with something to say.

The floral quality of Tipton's wines, characterized across her entire portfolio, is the result of the sandy loam Oz Clarke spoke of in his Sentinel interview. This sort of soil drains well and produces softer wines with controlled acidity and pronounced aromatics. These qualities appear prominently in her Picpoul.

Picpoul is an interesting grape--one of the thirteen permitted varietals in white Châteauneuf-du-Pape, used primarily as a blending component, often for its crisp bite. In these sandy soils, it is capable of—and excels at—being a single varietal showcase. Directly translated, Picpoul means lip stinger, but in Lodi the acids are held in check. Acquiesce's 2015 Picpoul shows a rounded, juicy compass of tropical flavors, tangerine to banana and pineapple. Although Tipton currently cultivates less than a hundred vines, what comes out the business end is a wine to rival any French Picpoul I've tried—certainly, the Languedoc estate that produce Picpoul as a stand-alone make steely, mineral-driven wines with considerably less weight.

Acquiesce Viognier (2014) is a closer counterpart to its Northern Rhône paradigm in the tiny appellations of Condrieu—it is plush and fragrant, filled with exotic mango, papaya and grapefruit notes. The 2015 we opened, having recently been slipped into that stylish Sabine glassware, was dealing with a bit of bottle shock—it was lighter and less beguiling on the nose.

Belle Blanc (2104) is her pretty baby, her homage, her tribute to the great estates of Châteauneuf-du-Pape in the Vaucluse department of southeastern France. Like these rare and majestic wines, Belle Blanc bursts with fruit and perfume, bright tones of yellow, a sweet, honeyed nose resplendent with lemon and pear; a succulent mouthful that is viscous and creamy and crisp nonetheless. She has, in effect, created a work of art that might easily be mistaken for its prototype, and without anything more than an excellent palate, an exemplary vineyard and a determination to succeed.

Opposite the "Before I Die..." board, there is a dictionary definition of Acquiesce painted high on the wall: "To surrender; to become quiet..."

Sue Tipton maintains that she and her husband thought of the name long before they thought of the winery—it is from the k.d. lang song, that, as far as I can figure out, is about strange sex.

But that doesn't matter; here, Acquiesce is about glorious wine, superb pairings with local products (one of Sue Tipton's most popular tasting room amenities) and fun conversation on the ground floor of the white wine revolution in Lodi.

If you must bring strange sex to the party, write on the wish board. k.d. will have to show up one of these afternoons.

12. THE HOUSE THAT CESARE BUILT

Robert and Peter Mondavi are to Lodi, CA what Bob Dylan is to Hibbing, MN: Local boys made good, but a long way from their home town.

The fact that the Mondavi brothers didn't move to Lodi until they were in grade school, and prior to that lived in Hibbing, MN, may add a weird twist to the analogy, but not enough to warrant devoting a full chapter to them—or so I imagined. For the most part, the Mondavis made their mark on Lodi by moving out of Lodi, to Napa, where the brothers, through publicized splits and tentative reconciliations, became ambassadors for the Napa appellation. But Woodbridge, the project through which Robert Mondavi was able to stock shelves with five dollar mass-produced wines from Lodi to to finance his real focus two hours west and ultimately sold to Constellation in a package deal worth a billion dollars (or, if you prefer, 200 million bottles of Woodbridge

White Zinfandel; roughly 13,000 times what Cesare paid for Charles Krug winery in 1948), struck me as the opposite of the sort of Lodi winemaker I wanted this book to celebrate. Besides, he died in 2008, eliminating a chance for that journalistic gem that brings a story to life: The current quote.

So, I leapfrogged him. His younger brother Peter was alive when I got to California, and he had at least studied wine at UC Berkeley— at the helm of Charles Krug, searching for brighter, contemporary wines, he introduced cold fermentation and sterile filtration techniques that revolutionized the way Californians produced white wine. But, again, Peter Mondavi's laser beam was aimed at Napa, not Lodi, and although he has probably used contract fruit from Lodi in producing the workhouse CK Mondavi label, the implosion of Charles Krug winery after the brothers' infamous 1965 split and the string of vintages produced in the wake—Robert Parker called the '90s batch indifferent, innocuous and collectively superficial—makes the Mondavi story more tragic than heroic.

Still, a quote from the surviving brother, a patriarchal figure who helped put California as a whole on the wine map, might not have gone astray in a comprehensive Lodi story.

And then, on February 20, while I was steeped in Lodi, sodden with it, right in the middle of it, he died. The morning I heard the news I was interviewing Sue Tipton at Acquiesce, and as her tasting room features a large chalkboard "Bucket List" that patrons fill out, I was able to write "Meet Peter Mondavi" and cross it out in the space of half an hour.

But it was a milestone and—as the florid hacks are wont to spout—the end of an era—and seemed like a significant blip on the Lodi radar. So I figured the least I could do was track down the house where the boys grew up and take an obligatory gawker photo and pay quiet homage to the Mondavi patriarch who had, in any case, been frustrating Italian well-wishers for the past couple of birthdays: The traditional salud, "Cento di questi giorni!—May you live a hundred years'"—imploded after 2014, the year the old crypt-keeper turned one hundred.

For coordinates to the house I had to rely on my Lodi keeper, Randy Caparoso, who directed me to Pine Street just west of downtown, where the Mondavi bungalow (with a pair of stone lions guarding the front porch) nestles comfortably about midway down the shaded block.

Apparently the lions were a later accessory, because they do not appear in the photo I came across showing a well-marbled Cesare with his arms draped around elementary-school-aged Robert and Peter, the latter dressed in those absurd woolen knickers that were the rage for boys in the United States after World War I. All three gents in the picture look into the camera lens with a sort of smug self-assuredness, fat and confident, and a presage for the eno-empire that was to follow. It is also symbolic that the father stands between his two sons, a buffer, a pillar of separation, a Wall of Alesia like the one dad's namesake Julius built in 52 BC.

These days, the old Mondavi house is occupied by Tony Segale, a man with the dubious honor of being Lodi's Best Sign Painter. Segale specializes in gold-leaf lettering signs, and among his more notable clients is The Cheesecake Factory, although a nearer and dearer golden sign advertises Michael David Winery on Highway 12. According to Segale, the only mementos the Mondavis left behind were vinegar barrels and a roll of film that, as it happens, contained nothing compromising or blackmail-able.

What's clear is that they left the town behind; both boys graduated from

Lodi High School and went briefly into the family grape business, and after convincing Cesare to purchase Charles Krug in 1943, set out to establish themselves as Napa icons. Robert Mondavi built his Oakville winery in the legendary To Kalon Vineyard after he was ousted from Krug, thus leaving the first ever winery in Napa to establish the valley's first large-scale winery since prohibition.

The Charles Krug story begins in 1861, when a 27-year-old Prussian immigrant recognized the Napa terroir for what it was—one of a select few plots upon the planet where the wine gods assembled all the rain and sunshine and soil required to make a product of true distinction. To the mix, Krug added some requisite human widgets—a cider press for the grapes and ideal rootstock for the territory and soon became the most influential winemaker in the New World. He died in 1892, and a couple of years later the winery was purchased by James Moffit Jr., who produced his own version of Krug wine until Prohibition; after that, the place fell into relative ruin until it was picked up by Cesare Mondavi, ostensibly at his sons' recommendation.

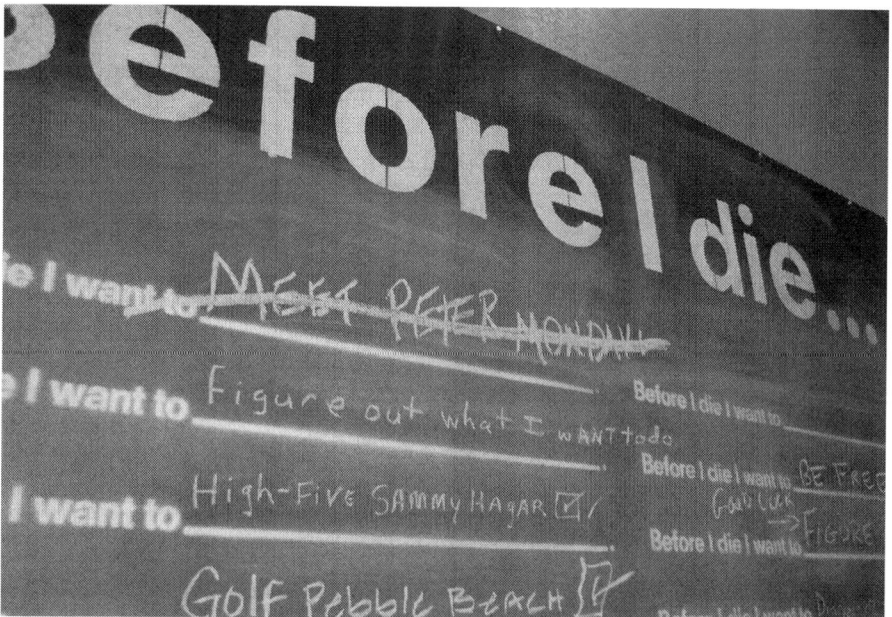

This was 1943, when Peter was stationed in England with the Army Air Corps for the remainder of World War II; he credits his brother Robert for having done the rehab work on the Krug estate, which still had damage from the earthquake of 1906:

"I have to give my brother, Bob, all the credit, because he put the winery in shape," Mondavi said in a 2014 interview. "The buildings had dirt floors, and the ceilings were gone. The vineyard had mostly grapes for bulk wine. Bob knew the Big Wheels, and somehow got the materials to rebuild. How he got it all with the war on, who knows?"

Peculiar, moving praise for a man with whom he'd come to physical blows over the direction of Charles Krug and effectively ousted from the operation. It may have been the insight of age—the interview, by St. Helena Star, was on the occasion of Peter Mondavi's hundred birthday. But it also ignores the contribution of Cesare, the patriarch, which I find even more peculiar. Although he was initially reluctant to purchase the Krug winery—he already owned two—his sons convinced him of the potential, and the record indicates that Moffitt sold to Cesare, despite other offers, because the San Francisco businessman recognized Cesare Mondavi as the same breed of visionary that Charles Krug had been.

In any case, although a condition of the purchase was that the estate be run by the boys, Cesare and his wife Rosa retained controlling interest in the winery until their deaths, 1959 and 1976 respectively. Cesare, it is said, had a 'quiet authority' that neither son dared challenge and Rosa, a semi-literate immigrant, was forced by circumstances to navigate legal matters and choosing between her sons.

Peter, the youngest (called "Babe"—a name he despised) won that round, leading to Robert's excommunication from Charles Krug, and although they made some tentative peace in later years, the rivalry between the brothers—for more insidious than Cain and Abel's—simmered for the rest of their lives. Peter ultimately won life's ultimately lottery prize, outliving his big brother by six years.

The Mondavi's tawdry melodrama played out in Napa, but the roots are on Pine Street in Lodi. No plaque memorializes the lion house, no statues stands in front of City Hall (also on Pine Street) and as the man who gilded the bear atop the Lodi arch, the current resident of the Mondavi home, Tom Segale may be the town's more valued resident.

But, Lodi's true treasure trove was evident in the tasting room at Acquiesce where I heard the news of Peter Mondavi's passing. Sue Tipton's agglomeration of bright, contemporary, cold-fermented Rhône whites. These wind up playing a more significant role in Lodi's wine aesthetics than all the Mondavi juice combined. It's an interesting footnote to his passing that throughout his life, his quest for better acres for better wine, some of the best land may have been nestling in his own backyard on Pine all along, right behind the house that Cesare built.

13. NATALIE SCOTTO: STREAMLINING THE LEVIATHAN

A few interesting things become obvious after a short conversation with Natalie Scotto. First, she doesn't operate on Scotto Time, that unique World Clock zone where everything is red-shifted forward ten or twenty or thirty minutes to fit rapid-fire schedule changes. Setting a meeting time with Natalie is different: If you say 11 AM, she's there en punto, every time.

Also, as a generally calm and introspective woman in an occasionally old-school Italian family overloaded with focused, jitterbug males, she is a unique puzzle piece that nonetheless fits in securely—her talents are a beautiful and strategic counterpoint to theirs.

Third, her legal name is Natalie Woods, which as a name comes with more baggage than a family of hyper-male Scotto brothers—she called her company 'J. Woods Beverage Group', explaining that her middle name, Jean, is a "J" name, and that to her, 'J. Woods' is sort of gender neutral and professional-sounding. And to an extent, I agree: J. Woods Beverage Group conjures up (to me) an image of a professional dude in a Jos. A. Bank wool suit sitting at a polished desk dotting his i's and crossing his t's. Natalie Woods Beverage Group makes me think of cute little Susie Walker sitting on Santa's lap, then growing up to be a bombastic beauty—in plural form.

Natalie Scotto-Woods is all that and more, and certainly no less. Number four in the Scotto birth order, she was the second one to join the family business, and even that happened, quite literally, by accident. Her father had a disagreement with a staircase, and the staircase won: She ended up as his driver throughout the healing process. "I felt like a gangster's driver," she laughs. "I never knew exactly where we were going or why, and I figured I was just there to push the gas pedal."

But if you learn the hard way (like I did) that driving anywhere in California means long sojourns in backed-up traffic, you also know that prolonged automotive clots generally results in long conversations. Over a number of congested afternoon, stuck on one of Northern California's arteries, Natalie learned an awful lot about the blood flowing though her own arteries—her family, her history, and of particular interest to her, what her father actually did for a living.

"It sounds strange," she admits, "But when I was growing up, I really was never sure what my dad did. I knew that it had to do with wine, but he had strange hours, worked out of our home office a lot and went off on trips. My friends all had fathers with more, sort of definable professions."

In fairness to A2, a lot of Natalie's childhood took place during a time when he was either out of the house or consulting for other wineries;

his hand was in many pies as he scrambled to establish the substructure of a company that his children would ultimately help expand, Natalie included. Her harpoon in that particular leviathan seems to have been forged in traffic, jam by jam, as she shuttled the wounded warrior between his various meetings. The upshot was a clearer—but by no means complete—view of what her role would be in the remarkable family dynasty, the great vinous behemoth that, whether or not the Scottos admit it, exists… and with growing proportions.

Natalie's was a baptism by fire. Or technically, by marriage. Her oldest brother Anthony got married and Natalie was called upon to do some temp work in the office while he was on an extended honeymoon—a sort of all-inclusive job without a description or formal introduction wherein she fielded phone calls from people making offers she couldn't even understand, let alone refuse. At first, it scared the sh*t out of her when people called and wanted to cut deals, sell this, buy that— she was a stranger in a strange land, but through the sheer weight of responsibility, she did not remain one for long. She handled the calls she could, negotiated when it made sense, solicited input from A2 when it didn't, learned the lexicon, figured out how to handle invoices and gradually, meticulously, began to get a handle on precisely what it was her father did for a living.

"It wasn't a cookie-cutter job, that's for sure," Natalie shares. "Nothing you can stamp with a paragraph on a resumé. At the time, I didn't figure I was cut out for that sort of lifestyle—I had just spent four years at UC Santa Barbara studying sociology and education, and I was sort of geared up for precisely a cookie-cutter profession, like teaching. My professors were pushing me toward grad school, and that's pretty much where I saw my future. What working in the wine industry entails is a life without routine. And I like routine."

But, in her mind, she owed her father a term of repayment: Thanks to him, she'd graduated college debt free and had spent a summer in Italy on the family dime. So, she took on the paper-pushing duties and the chauffeur duties, and by the time A3 returned from his honeymoon, she had begun to see a missing denominator in the Scotto equation:

Distribution, especially in Northern California.

An essential to any winery's formula is accessibility of product, and with the expanding portfolio of labels for which Scotto Family Cellars was responsible, getting shelf space and store placement was becoming an imperative. Making wine involves a certain amount of throwing caution to the wind, but selling that wine is a whole different ball game: You've got to harness that wind and convince customers sitting inside life's stadium that they want to drink it. That involves a unique skill set, and two years ago, when her father and brother approached her to build a distribution network in Northern California, in part to cushion her family's brands and in part because they sensed she would be good at it.

Before she agreed, however, she had a trio of non-negotiable conditions:

First, the company had to be based on a commercially sound business plan; second, it had to encompass a roster of like-minded people, both as clients and as representatives, which in brief means that integrity is bigger than the dollar. And the third condition was but a mono-word synopsis of Condition #2, a concept understood by Italian gangster drivers and Italian wine people alike: Honor.

So with those contract riders in place, her family purchased a distribution company called Eagle Rock, and while maintaining her role at Scotto Cellars managing exports, compliance and wine and cider tasting event planning, Natalie agreed to take the reins, renaming it after herself—sort of.

I sat down with Natalie at eleven en punto inside the upstairs all-purpose room at the Scotto's Cluff Avenue winery in Lodi. We rapped for a long time about the whole state of affairs, her family, her job, her outlook, her future. She is a Scotto in every sense of the word, displaying the charm, energy and humility that I read as characteristic of the clan.

When I hung around with the eldest Scotto scion, A3, I was struck with the paternal attitude he adopted when dealing with his siblings; that might be a natural birthright of primogeniture, and I found it touching. But, equally touching is Natalie's perhaps unconscious maternal predisposition that bubbles to the surface when she discusses her brothers—she looks out for them, scraps with them, does not suffer much backseat nonsense that might cause her to pull the car over to the side of the road.

Not that the true family matriarch, dear Gracie Scotto—who held down the fort through A2's many masterpieces and missteps—is anything less than all encompassing as a mother figure; the short time I was able to spend with her was glorious. She is, in every sense of her name, grace. Every Scotto, including A2, acknowledges her role as the true hero of the Scotto story.

But Natalie possesses that grace as well, wrapped inside the front of a shrewd businesswoman—probably shrewder than she originally gave herself credit for. She'd have made a good teacher, too, and God protect the student that thought he could slip something by her. She has shows uncanny insight into her family's individual fortitudes and foibles, perks and quirks, pluses and pockmarks and she rattled off a summation of her brothers with dead fire accuracy.

Number One Son Anthony, she notes, is a true visionalist. A hyper-energy salesman that would have made a sensational history teacher, (as much as I thought that she would have):

"He's got a brain wired for sales," she maintains. "And all the lateral thinking skills that requires. I've never seen anybody who can be in so many places at the same time, not even my dad. But with him, it's organized and disciplined chaos. He's really a phenomenal leader because he teaches by example, not by lecture."

Of Paul, the brother she claims is most like her in an approach to the wine industry, she say, "Paul is fun—he's approachable and authentic, but highly technical. He does nothing without research. You find something you need for a dollar, I guarantee that Paul will find it for 99¢.

But, with these respects paid, she owns an ephemeral sort of attachment to her brother Michael perhaps unmatched in the others: "We're closest in age and went through a lot of the same things at home; we had the same friends growing up and we both have—to some extent—a "go with the flow" attitude. With Michael, that's a feature of hard work; he's there, where he needs to be, every day without fail. He's the go-to guy—

box sizes, bottle weights, that sort of stuff. Paul is the technical whiz, but Michael takes care of the details."

For her father, Natalie reserves the review that is the most poignant, and the one that may reflects most upon her own character: "I used to hear him in the morning, up ridiculously early, loud music playing, and I never really gave him credit for the depth of his knowledge—how his environment was perfectly suited to his performance. Which is almost always superb. I remember him trying to bring in some sea containers of wine from Argentina and I kicked and screamed, thinking he was out of his mind. Looking back on it, I think he might have been testing me, seeing how I would react to such a risky move; anyway, I don't think we wound up with that wine so on some level, he must have agreed with me."

Her loyalty to the cause, however, both genetic and professional, is perhaps better illustrated by her reaction when we discussed the years that her father was gone, when there was no heavy metal at five in the morning, no long stints in the home office, no mentor riding shotgun and talking genealogy during traffic jam. It was tough on all the kids, she says, but on her and Michael especially, because they were still at home and had to field the inquiries. Tough on Gracie, of course, but in the end, she had the adult perspective that might have been still beyond the kids. And Gracie forgave him, quicker, perhaps, than he has forgiven himself.

Has Natalie? "He's human, we all make mistakes. He's admitted his and he's apologized. I accept it, and we move forward."

The true test, I figured, was to press my luck and the propriety and the situation's delicacy and and ask her if she'd forgive her own husband Josh—a great dude who fits into the family seamlessly—for the same transgression. And she doesn't miss a beat: "Of course," she says. "And I've told him so."

See, to me, that's class squared. That's grace under pressure. Or better: That's behaving with honor even when those around you, those you love the most, do not. And the ability—the inclination—to do this becomes the test of any true teacher, whether in a classroom or a boardroom: Leading by example.

14: MOHR-FRY IS NOT A FAST FOOD ORDER

Mr. Mohr was not available, so I interviewed Mr. Fry. And then another Mr. Fry entered the room. More Fry.

Now that the inevitable, irascible and wholly irresistible puns are dispensed with, I will address a couple of old-school farmers who are part of a daisy chain of Lodi agriculture that pre-dates the Civil War.

The Mohr family, great-great grandsires of Bruce Fry, the current and 5th generation of Mohr-Fry Ranch stepped off a whaling ship in San Francisco in the 1850s and decided to trade surf for turf. He began farming on a Spanish land grant in Mt. Eden, where a quick Google Map search reveals that Mohr St. is today a prominent thoroughfare. This fellow, Cornelius, had a son called William who seems to have been the Mohr with a knack for novelty—he expanded the roster of row crops to include tomatoes, sugar beets and wheat, but especially, he began to experiment with hybridizing irises and became internationally renowned for his work in horticultural research.

Pioneering agriculture was, in fact, the very thing that brought me to

Mohr-Fry Ranch on a cold day in February, where I sat in study of Jerry Fry and his son Bruce. They are a couple of congenial roughnecks on the exterior—Jerry is a tough old gleaner with hands like potent leather implements and eyes that have a permanent sunshine squint, even inside. Bruce, bearded, leaner, is a younger version of the same, where the squint is nascent, but well along the path. These are the faces of farmers—proud, determined, weathered and intense—but it is the cogs whirring behind these faces that are most intriguing. Stevia, the pet zero-calorie sweetener of the all-natural crowd—of which California has more than its share? That was an innovation spearheaded by Jerry Mohr, who planted the first commercial stevia crop in the United States—a hundred acres, back in the 1990s. And that doesn't amount to a hill of beans compared to the Mohr-Fry hill of beans: The ranch is among the premiere sources for heirloom dry beans in the United States, offering 27 varieties, most of which neither you nor I have ever heard of. Arikara Yellow? Jacob's Cattle Gold? Hutterite? Old vine Zinfandel is cool, but 'Black Valentine' rules your face off.

The Old Vine Zin keeps the lights on, though, and you get the impression that Jacob's Cattle Gold and Eye of the Goat are the fifth generation's hybridized irises.

Mohr-Fry Ranches currently has about 300 acres to grape, and the muster is as multifarious as the heirloom beans. And the list of Mohr-Fry clients is all over the map—literally.

"The tail can't wag the dog," Jerry Fry explains, summarizing the business philosophy that has sustained the family concern for a century and a half: "It's not about pushing paper, it's a personal thing. You have people in, say, Delaware, looking for quality wine. My name won't be on the label, and Lodi may not appear on the label, but I still have the obligation to provide the highest quality fruit for the product."

That's an end game and a process, and I must say, even though his office was decked with awards and commendations, testimonials and magazine clippings, Fry looked manifestly uncomfortable sitting in a study discussing his farm—he looked like he'd rather be out in it, up to his elbows in sandy loam and microbiota. As some older gentlemen will reminisce about the salad days of their youth, Fry talks about growing that salad—how he went through phases of irrigation eureka moments, describing the progressive changes in technique, from digging furrows, to spoon feeding vines in the early Seventies, to drip irrigation, to running pipes underground, to setting up sprinklers—not necessarily in that order and not necessarily as independent strategies, but as a reminder of the myriad decisions a farmer intent on keeping up with technology while respecting tradition must face every day.

"Generalizations are easy," he points out. "Nailing them down is hard. We are huge proponents of sustainable agriculture—a term we prefer to organic. 'Sustainable' looks at everything; the environment and the soil and the social aspects like as community and employees and economic sustainability."

Nowhere is this ideology more succinctly codified than in the volume that Bruce Fry soon brought into the room and whumped down on the desk like a phone book. Bruce is the face of the next generation of Fry farm folk—tan, rugged and brimming with agricultural ethics, ideas about biodiversity, pushing the three E's of sustainable farming—environment, social equity, and economics. He's a proud to be a founding member of a local movement that have seen these ideals codified in a book so revolutionary that it has been used as template for systemized, sustainable growing in other regions across California. The Lodi Rules includes a fully auditable set of viticultural standards—101 in total—that balance environmental, social, and economic goals. Established in 2005, it was designed to communicate members' commitment to sustainable agriculture to wineries and the general public, and is considered by its founders to be a work in progress. Lodi Rules committee chair Chris Storm summarizes the program's evolution this way:

"The Rules were revised in 2013 to place a greater emphasis of scientific rigor of the standards while making the program more adaptable to business management goals. Our intention is to keep the Rules the pre-eminent certification program in California."

The family that tills together is still together. Beside son Bruce, Jerry Fry's sister is the VP of Administration and his brother-in-law is the CFO.

But Jerry spreads the love throughout the place, saying, "We're concerned about health and community and want our workers to feel good, and feel like they are part of the family. We have one gentleman who's worked for the family for over 65 years — that tells you something. It's about communication, trusting people and giving them reign so that they are proud of what they're involved in."

The overarching sense of a Mohr-Fry dynasty extends to customers as well, and he's as protective of his brood as any patriarch. This includes the big fish like Gallo, Treasury and Constellation as well as the minnows and smelt; Abundance Vineyards, St. Amant, Balistreri. They're not all in Lodi, and those that aren't don't always mention that a lot of the richness in their wine actually does come from Lodi—the worst kept secret in California. But Jerry Fry holds all of his buyers in equal esteem, because they are all essential constituents to his success, to longevity of the ranch and the health of the business.

That's a new view of sustainability—a revolutionary interpretation. It extends the concept of renewable beyond the cellar, beyond the soil, beyond the cellar, beyond the produce and into the keeping the name intact.

Because after all, few of these old-school Lodi farmers would disagree that preserving the family legacy is the biggest fish of all to fry.

15. MARKUS NIGGLI: NOUVEAU NICHE

A tall, buff, Teutonic, well-spoken European wine pro in his early forties? Making unique wines that can, in ways, re-define his appellation? Put this dude in any tasting room in any wine country in the world and you'd assume the lines would be out the door. Yet when I asked Markus Niggli how many customers Borra Vineyards drew last weekend?

"Seven or eight."

That figure does not have a couple of zeros after it in case you are reading it as a typo—leading one to all sorts of bizarre conclusions, none of them accurate. In fact, the tasting room is out of the way, and it's not huge; Niggli's personal brand is something of a Borra Vineyards afterthought and I did not ask the question during the Lodi tourist season such as it may or may not exist.

Like the locale, some of Niggli's varietal choices are a bit off the beaten wine trail path. Kerner, for example. Or Bacchus. How do you lure non-geeks into your tasting room, right in the middle of Old Vine Zintopia, with obscure Swiss and German white wines?

Apparently, that remains an open question.

Kerner and Bacchus are cold-climate grapes developed during the last century and they are well suited to the winter wonderland of Germany, Austria and Alto Adige in Northern Italy. They are a strange, but ultimately functional choice for the Mediterranean climate of Lodi. Kern is a cross between Riesling and a red varietal called Trolligner; Bacchus was a hybrid created by viticulturalist Peter Morio at the Geilweilerhof Institute for Grape Breeding in the Palatinate, a three-way blend of a Sylvaner, Riesling and Müller-Thurgau. Neither offers any genuine synergy with Riesling—that is, a sum greater than the whole of their parts—and likely couldn't: Riesling is, without question, the most versatile grape in the world. The crossbreeds were an attempt to 'fix' some of the limitations of the parent grapes. Bacchus, for example, has a high must weight and can ripen in climates where Riesling struggles. Kerner, which at one time was Germany's 3rd most planted grape, offers resistance to downy mildew, powdery mildew and botrytis and it produces an abundant crop. It has been used as a sort of the poor volk's Riesling, Kerner as the poor volk's Müller-Thurgau, with Bacchus more or less bringing up the rear.

But these grapes can at least bright and crisp and unique and Aryan, so along with Gewürztraminer and Riesling, they held immense appeal to winemaker Markus Niggli:

"I'm from Switzerland," he told me over a glass of Nimmo—a blend of Kerner, Gewürztraminer, Riesling and Bacchus—"These are grapes I grew up with, grapes I identify with."

It probably helped that he could identify them—there aren't many grown in California, obviously, and across the state, all four Nimmo grapes combined probably represent less than ten thousand acres, and most of that is planted to the sort of perennial Pacific pet-project, Riesling.

Eight of those acres—the ones key to Niggli's story—were planted in by Bob and Mary Lou Koth, about a quarter of the 26 acres that had been in their family since the early 1960s. They had been primarily Chardonnay and Zinfandel growers until their daughter daughter Ann-Marie, now a German language teacher at Lodi High School, returned from a Fulbright scholarship in Germany with a roster of new favorite wines. In 1994, they planted an experimental 'German Collection' that included, along with the Nimmo quartet, Rieslaner, Schonberger, Ehrenfelser, Kanzler and Oraniensteiner and Weisser Burgunder. There are also some red varietals planted: Blaufränkisch*, Zweigelt, Dornfelder and Spätburgunder—a German clone of Pinot Noir.

* As a brief digression, if I suggested that Blaufränkisch is the single most expensive varietal currently produced in California, you might think it was another typo, but according to the annual Grape Crush Report released by the USDA, Blaufränkisch went for $3,400 a ton— the only red grape to break the $3 k ceiling.

Niggli's winemaking story didn't begin until he was thirty; he has a business degree in tourism and marketing, which may in fact make the relative scarcity of tasting room patrons even more ironic. He worked for Swiss Railway and American Airlines, and in the course of his world travels—a perk of the position—he began to explore wine regions and learn what people were trying to express in their wines through regional traditions, indigenous grapes and personal imperatives. In 2004, he decided he wanted to learn not only what winemakers did, but how they did it, and without having banked the quarter million dollars it takes to get an enology degree at UC Davis, he headed to Perth, Australia, where he spend a year studying viticulture until the money he did have ran out, then headed to Napa to look for work… any work.

"I couldn't find anything for a long time, even though I'd just come from Swan Valley where I worked tasting rooms days and studied viticulture nights. Apparently I still wasn't qualified for a $10 per hour job changing hoses."

Ultimately, he fell into a consulting gig in which he was responsible of shipping grapes to the East Coast, and in that role, met a few of the winemakers out there that remain part of his winemaking program today. His private label "Markus Joey Insieme" (2014) is a blend of California Torrontés and North Carolina Riesling. Insieme means together in Italian and Joey means Joey Medaloni, a former nightclub owner who, like Niggli, began making wine in his thirties. The spec sheet refers to Insieme as "a worthy substitute for a morning Bloody Mary," which must be unique in the annals of wine tasting notes.

Unique is the name of the game, of course, and the wash of wine that I sampled with Markus that lonely afternoon in the tasting room reflected every bit of that, some with more success than others. The problem with Kerner is that it can produce wines so sharp you can clean your teeth with it, and often does not provide sufficient fruit to sufficiently liven up the party. Kerner-heavy wines tend to be high in minerality, austere and frosty, often strikingly acidic and Niggli's tendency to pick grapes early, sometimes at 21° Brix, amplifies this. Despite the use of native yeasts in his fermentation tanks, these wines are highly stylized works of contemporary art. The labels themselves are as well, having been designed by students at the University of the Pacific in Stockton— students who, Niggli says, "have their passions in the right place."

At my request, Markus walked me through a year-by-year overview of Lodi's changing terroir, which he has followed with the keen sense of a climatologist. The rap offered insight not only into some of the unusual flavors he seeks and elicits, but why, of all the terroirs in all the gin joints in all the world, he settled down in this one.

Since he began making wine at Borra in 2006, Niggli has kept obsessive records of horticultural events at the vineyards he relies upon, and he sees patterns that show some drastic shifts in climate—tangible stuff, tasteable stuff, not charts from a NASA site. All vineyard managers have noticed a red shift in the growing season; bud break occurring earlier and earlier, flowering following suit at a quickened pace, and grapes that may reach optimum ripeness as much as a month earlier today than they did twenty years ago.

"And it's not just here," Niggli points out. "Look at the changing face of Spanish red wines. Garnacha—today, it's fruit forward, high acid, less hang time. Here, in 2013, we started picking Zinfandel at the beginning of September rather than the end, and in 2014, when we had a warm winter and a dry, hot summer, we brought in the first trucks of Zinfandel on August 20. In 2015, we actually began to harvest the Syrah before the white grapes."

He further describes 2015 as an early bloom, with a cold snap during flowering leading to an initial loss of crop of around 20%. Then the drought kicked in, and the season progressed well with great flavor intensity. But, Niggli notes, a significant downside to warmer winters is that many insects that normally would have perished now survive and eradication programs are becoming progressively less effective. The drive toward organic production limits the pesticides that can be used, and many of the natural ones are not potent enough to get the job done.

A bug boom and the resultant explosion of insect-borne is a reality which those who enjoy the benefits of a milder climate will need to contend.

A niche may be literally defined as one of two things: An ornamental recess or a distinct segment of a given market. In this case, during my visit, the tasting room at Borra was both. Sort of cluttered, but not with patrons—with cases and knick-knacks and awards; it's cozy like a Swiss chalet.

Outside, Borra sprawls across two vineyards and many decades, with origins spanning back to Benevagiena in the Italian Piedmont. That was the home of Stephen Borra's maternal grandfather Giuseppe Manassero who emigrated to Lodi over a century ago and set up shop on Armstrong Road, where the winery sits today.

Stephen has owned the place since 1966, and prior to hiring winemaker Markus Niggli in 2006, the family focused on Barbera and Carignane and, in 1992, after purchasing an additional 200 acres planted to Old Vine Zinfandel and Chardonnay, further expanded into Merlot, Viognier, Cabernet Sauvignon and Syrah. These remain the core varietals at Borra and as it happens, Niggli excels in producing them. His Fusion Red 2009—a proprietary blend of Syrah, Petite Syrah, Zinfandel and Alicante Bouchet took home double gold at the 2012 San Francisco Chronicle Wine Competition; 2008 Fusion Red also found a spot on the Wall Street Journal's Annual Dozen top wines, although ironically, the accompanying blurb mentions that the wine "regularly fills the tasting room" (!) Apparently, either they are sold out of the '08 or I caught the crew on the wrong day.

Either way, recombinant, Borra and Niggli are steeped in tradition while embracing the changes in climate and tastes, terroir and fashion, style and substance.

Niggli's personal portfolio, produced by under the Markus label, have been described as feminine, but I don't see it—I see, perhaps, the opposite: These wines are intense and angular, cool and daring... just like the winemaker.

16. THE FLUID PRICELESS AND KEYS TO THE KINGDOM

"The thing that hath been, it is that which shall be; and that which is done is that which shall be done: and there is no new thing under the sun." - Ecclesiastes 1: 9

Lodi survived seedless table grape revolution; it survived the phylloxera plague that decimated Napa in the 1880s and it survived the Panic of 1907 when a number of local banks and businesses went belly-up. So it's no surprise that Prohibition was but another smudge on the vast vanity mirror of life—Lodians wiped it away and moved forward.

According to the Lodi Sentinel of Nov. 9, 1920:

'Wine is being made under government supervision and restriction, with internal revenue agents on the job and the delicious product under lock and key so that not a drop of the fluid priceless is sold for beverage purposes. If all this wonderful wine is to be used at the altar, there is enough in storage in Lodi to last all the religionists until the waters of the Mokelumne River flow eastward—and that will be some considerable last. Some of this liquid will be used, mayhap, in the making of patent medicines, for there are yet ills of the body that require a mild tonic, the like of which is contained only in the juice of the Lodi Zinfandel.'

Furthermore, despite the Eighteenth Amendment, which pulled the bottom from beneath the American wine industry, the people Lodi not only breezed through, they were actually happier and richer and healthier than before. Two years after the gushing 'fluid priceless' notice, on November 23, 1922 the Lodi Sentinel reported: 'The joy of living in a community of health and prosperity has knocked the 'die' out of Lodi. There have been no deaths in the Lodi section for several days, according to local undertakers. The only death reported was the death of Old Man Pessimism at the big meeting of the Lodi Realty Board Monday night. Lodi people are too busy preparing for the grape season of 1923 and are too happy and contented with living in the finest section of California to even think about death.'

One of the then-technological marvels that ensured continued prosperity was the refrigerated rail car, known as the 'reefer'. First conceived during the Civil War, the idea piggybacked on the development of whistle stops and rail towns across the country and was intended as a conveyance for perishable items between farm and marketplace. J.B. Sutherland was granted the first refrigerator car patent on November 26, 1867, but the railroads were slow to hop on board: The first generation of reefers were damp and musty, cost twice as much as standard box-cars and contained less overall space due to insulation and bunkers. Beef packers led the charge, and in those days, capital-poor railroads did not own many of the cars they hauled; they charged a fee for companies moving goods along the normal exchange. This began to change after

1901, when consumer demands for fresh, refrigerated products made the reefer a sounder investment, and by the time Prohibition rolled into town, the East Coast market for refrigerated California table grapes was already established. The Volstead Act had a loophole allowing home winemakers to produce up to 200 gallons a year, and this was a new, and shortly massive, niche within the grape transport business. Lodi—then as now a grape production powerhouse—cashed in.

The centerpiece of the enterprise was the most glamorous freight car fleet in the country—shiny yellow boxes with steel underframes, painted with colorful slogans and logos, 35 feet long and capable of carrying 30 tons of grapes. At each end was a bunker with a hatch, and the compartment was filled with ice at stations along the way. These pit stops were similar to those at the Indy 500 in terms of activity; while the bunkers were iced by one crew of men, another climbed beneath the train to inspect cars for mechanical defects, adjusting brakes and making minor repairs. A third force worked alongside the train, checking each car against the consignment orders held at that point, carding the cars to be cut out and sent to the hold track for diversion.

Among the more interesting devices that reefers employed were a series of fans to blow cold air from the ice bunkers over the produce. Axle-driven, forced-air circulation fans were in general use until 1904, when a refrigerator car with a friction driven blower was exhibited at the St. Louis World's Fair.

How this somewhat graphic description of a Prohibition-era reefer and the quote from Ecclesiastes ties into the story of the old Roma winery will shortly be revealed.

Denis's Country Kitchen is one of those dear old rural diners where everybody is best friends with everybody else, where the coffee is awful and slammed nonetheless; where the bathroom is around back and where the short-order cooks look like ex-cons—tough, grey-haired old dudes with tattoos and muscles—and the waitresses are small-town pretty and keep your awful cup of coffee topped up without you even noticing it.

This is where I was supposed to meet David Sproul, owner of property where the old Roma Winery once sat, and even though the Roma Winery closed in 1952, and has been many things to many people and many wineries to many vintners since, everybody still calls it the old Roma Winery.

Old records show that it was once a clearing house of Flame Tokay grapes, listed as "Tokay strippings", and they were sold based on sugar content. 20% sugar went for $8.50 a ton and 26% sugar (loosely corresponding to what the wine world might call 27 Brix) fetched a whopping $11.50 per ton.

But wine was the stock in trade for the building, constructed in 1917 by the Scatena family, who owned the Roma Winery in hilly Healdsburg and decided to relocate to Lodi where the flat countryside made expansion easier. The winery was purchased by John Celia in 1922, who obtained the necessary permits to produce 'medicinal' and sacramental wine, and who also shipped huge quantities of grape juice to New York, no doubt with the same wink and nod of another Lodi winery, who wrote, "We knew that a lot of the juice we shipped east was destined to become bootleg hooch, but figured it wasn't our problem."

After Prohibition ended, Celia began a concentrated expansion of Roma Winery, and included the first cement fermenting tanks in the state, capable of processing 156,000 gallons of wine at a time, and cooperage to store 5,000,000 gallons. It was, therefore, not only the biggest winery in Lodi, it was the biggest winery in California.

Celia sold the Roma Winery label and the property to Schenley Distillers in 1942, who a decade later, sold it to Felix Costa and John Graffigna, who changed the name to Mid-Valley Winery in 1952. In 1971, it was purchased by Fred C. Sproul and later taken over by his son David Sproul, who in turn leases the winery buildings and office space to Scotto Family Cellars.

Getting a handle on all this history, with all its convoluted wheeling's and dealings, owners and vintners, dreams and dynasties, characters and caretakers, was the very reason I sat in a cramped diner booth, listening to David Sproul and drinking endless refills of Denis' Country Kitchen.

The history was interesting and is summarized above and the future is being designed by David with a desire for continuity. A spiritual man who began our diner meal by saying grace and insisting that I join in (I was happy to), he said, "I'm only a steward of this land; God owns it."

The past had been laid out, David was eager to tell me about his latest enterprise, and that where the Biblical quote kicks in, which is something he should appreciate. He is marketing a low-cost, small-space air conditioner the runs on penlight batteries. It is essentially a plastic bucket you fill with frozen jugs of water with a proprietary chemical added to ensure a longer freeze time. Then a circulation fan blows a stream of air over the ice, and the unit is capable of keeping an enclosed space cool and breezy for an extended period.

Sound familiar? J.B. Sutherland's refrigerator car patent expired more than a century ago, so it's not a legal thing. Some folks might call it reinventing the wheel, but here in Lodi, it is to be considered a respect for local tradition and a nod to an inspirational verse from another book of proverbs, Nation's Business:

"If it isn't broke, don't fix it..." - Bert Lance, May, 1977

17. SHAWN THE FLOP AND AL THE WOP

Napa pickpockets tourists, Sonoma tolerates tourists, Lodi pines for tourists. That's the basic conceptual distillation with which my Lodi month out has left me.

In the alley behind my temporary shelter on S. School St., Shawn is a homeless kid without much shelter and frankly, in Lodi, without much need for it. It's sixty degrees and sunny in February, and he has a little corner near a Christian donation center and he sleeps behind a utility box on a donated mattress and under another donated mattress propped up by the utility box. He has a ton of worthless little possessions, mostly in the form of tangled wiry things—ear buds, computer cable, bungee cords—and every time I pass him when heading from my car to my door, he's arranging them in neat piles, after which he arranges them again, only this time differently. I stop and rap about nothing, which is his favorite topic, and I bring him food and cigarettes, not because I am a

121

Good Samaritan particularly, but because he has a place in this narrative and I don't want his story to be something for nothing. If I had to guess I'd say he is around twenty-five years old, and there is a Salvation Army nearby where he could crash if he wanted to, but he doesn't want to. He doesn't want to work either—I found someone willing to offer him a job pushing a broom in a warehouse and he came up with all sorts of impossible contract riders, like his availability window, only (for some inscrutable reason) between 5:00 and 7:30 AM.

I got into town on Super Bowl Sunday, which was happening a hundred miles to the southwest in Santa Clara. The Sacramento airport was jamming and the local newspapers all had stories about San Francisco sweeping the streets of homeless people, herding them like longhorns into tent cities far from the downtown staging area—called "Super Bowl City" even though Levi Stadium is an hour's drive south, even without the traffic jams. Football fans, it was reasoned, would spend before-and-after Superbucks in San Francisco listening to Alicia Keys and One Republic, zip line down CBS Sports' replica Golden Gate Bridge and drink copious amounts of Bud Lite—toasting fifty years of Super Bowls.

Such loyal NFL patrons, it was reasoned, willing to shell out thousands for the experience, should not have to be made uncomfortable by a view of how the other half forages.

Ironically, the Super Bowl winds up being only the third most widely viewed annual sporting event in the world, outpaced by a couple shindigs that most Americans have never heard of: The UEFA Champions League final and El Clásico in Spain.

I'd be willing to bet rent money that most Americans have never heard of the annual Lodi Wine & Chocolate Festival, which this year happened a full week after Super Bowl Sunday, no doubt so as not to steal any of its thunder. It's a fun event, nineteen years running, in which the bulk of Lodi's wineries feature "decadent pairings and treats" and people come from all over Northern California to check out the fare. Tickets are $65 each on the day of the event, and for that kind of money, and eager to flash Lodi's beauty without her slip showing, the Police Department took a cue from the brass in San Francisco and descended on Lodi's indigent population, arresting violators, offering mental health services, herding the homeless into shelters.

In the aftermath, The Lodi Sentinel reported, "City workers removed three full-sized dump trucks full of garbage left behind" but I suspect that one man's garbage is another man's collection of ear buds and co-axial cables.

In any case, by the morning of the event, Shawn and all his little meaningless, meaningful tchotchkes had vanished.

Twenty miles northwest of Lodi there is a landmark that is just as unaccountable as Shawn's employment demands and his trinket hoard: The town of Locke. It's not a tent city and it's not a shelter, but it was, in fact, built by homeless people after a fire in nearby Walnut Grove obliterated their neighborhood. That hood happened to be Chinatown, and Locke's founding fathers were all Chinese.

Locke was built in 1915 and then as now, covers fourteen total acres.

That snippet of background might serve as nothing but an historical tidbit, except that Locke has been left virtually unchanged since the day it was invented. It still operates like a normal podunk village with a population of under a hundred; there are strange little shops and unpainted antique façades and old buildings leaning at crazy angles, threadbare and hideworn and all those other adjectives you'd use to describe a wannabe tourist trap that these days seems to trap primarily biker gangs. On the day I made my pilgrimage to Locke, the place looked like Carbonville in The Wild One, with hoards of Harleys, scads of scoots, passels of panheads all descending on the towns one dusty main street, mostly big dudes with mamas in various incarnations of skankery, all looking for beer and some Sunday chillaxing.

It's a fair assumption that the bikers had not roared into town to visit Joe Stroong's Chinese School, to get acupunctured or moxibutioned at the Chinese Medicine Shop or to genuflect before the twin busts of Sun-Yat-Sen and Confucius that sit beneath the "Welcome to Locke" sign. They were here for the town's iconic dive bar, the Aristotelian archetype for every dive bar in every small town everywhere—a place one free-associates with being loud, embarrassingly drunk and inappropriate—a joint that goes by the unlikely un-P.C. name of Al the Wop's.

I wasn't at the mile-long wooden bar within the cavernous Al's for sixty

SHAWN THE FLOP AND AL THE WOP

seconds when an older gentleman beside me, perhaps in an effort to impress his equally-older date with arcane knowledge, announced that the term "wop" began as an acronym for "without papers," an official-sounding ethnic slur to recognize the illegal status of many early Italian immigrants. It happens, though, that I once did a documentary on Italian immigrants and remember that this urban myth was busted—the term is actually a play on the Italian word 'guappo' to describe a slick thuggish dude, used then like "Guido" is today. Still, picking a fight with an old man in a biker bar wouldn't have ended well for either of us, so I nodded politely and commented on the row of ancient Acme beer cans lining the shelf above the cash register, Wylie Coyote's brand.

The original Al the Wop was Al Adami. He came from another nearby rivertown, Ryde—a place that today demonstrates a similar distain for propriety in business names; there's a downtown hawker of angleworms and minnows to fisherman called "The Master Baiter." In 1934, Al took over the 13943 Main Street bar from Lee Bing, and thus became the only non-Chinese tenant in town, developing a reputation for bizarre behavior, including stirring female patrons' drinks with his finger, cutting neckties off of male patrons because they were too formal, and—in a tradition that remains in full force today—taping dollar bills all over the fifteen-foot-high ceiling. The old dude's old date piped up with a story of the IRS once doing a Black Rebels Motorcycle Club-like end run on Al's and forcing them to count all the dollar bills for tax purposes.

If I suspected the story might be as apocryphal as the wop story, she confirmed it by saying, "Turns out there was over a million dollars up there..."

There are somewhat less than a million dollar bills on the pressed tin panels overhead at Al's, but there are a lot of them. There's also a NASCAR race on the TV above the bar and big, leather-jacketed

Johnny Strablers all along the bar stools, some with club color patches, some looking more like weekend warriors out for cruises on expensive, non-chopped motorcycles, but most of them at Al's for a dose of the house specialty:

"Steak sandwich," the bartender assured me, so I ordered one and instantly received a disclaimer: "But it isn't a sandwich any more. You still get the steak and the bread, only not on the same plate."

Whatever. While I was waiting, however, I noticed that another popular item being carted by, a big plate of pickled banana peppers served with a side of Jif's Peanut Butter and something that looked like apricot jam. I did the requisite "WTF?" and the bartender assured me, "It's really, really good!"

And when the signature steak sandwich showed up, all the quirks that makes Al the Wops a quirk among quirks, which out-quirks the quirkiest gin joint in all the towns in all the world became self-evident. It is served with a side of grilled 'shrooms, two slices of toasted bread (on a separate plate, as promised) and a jar of Jif's Peanut Butter and a crock of something that looked like—and was—apricot jam.

So that's the takeaway (no pun) from Al the Wops: The life-lesson, the upshot, the meat 'n' potatoes: Everything, whether it is hot peppers, steak, french fries, or hamburgers, or fish tacos, or meat 'n' potatoes, goes better with PB&J.

At least, that's how every item on the menu is served.

Patrick

The road back to Lodi takes some interesting sprawls and swivels through Delta country; there are small fishing villages along the Sacramento River, many backed by acres of fecund farmland in full production, many with signs out front in support of "Stop the Tunnels"—a statewide coalition to stop the construction of $50 billion twin tunnels that would send more water to agribusiness and oil corporations at the expense of taxpayers. There are broad expanses of wetlands circled by waterfowl; hunting must be a riot up here despite the PETA purity manifested by a lot of Californians. Delta wine country is a whole different beast, layered with some of the most fertile soil on the planet and populated by vines and vintners that have learned to deal with wet feet despite many old-school assurances that the best wines come from poor, non-irrigated soils. The backdrop to the farmland, vivid or veiled depending on the day, are the Sierra Nevada mountains—they're snow-capped, which I'm told is unusual to see and the result of El Niño weather patterns. I'm such a flatlander that I thought the distant line of white was unusual, low-hanging clouds, and it took a week or so before I got used to the

127

comfortable idea that wherever you go in San Joaquin county, Big Momma Sierra always has your back.

Yellow mustard plants everywhere, in drainage ditches, between vine rows, bright and showy on the median of Highway 5. It's edible from phloem to flower, and is (surprisingly) 25% protein.

The last time I saw my man Shawn behind the apartment, I shared some protein with him in the form of a chicken I roasted and couldn't finish; this time, hoping that he had returned from his exile off Main Street, I brought him a peanut butter and Ribeye sandwich from Al's. No such luck, but there was another guy there, a wild-eyed dude named Patrick who told me he was an artist, and when I acknowledged that it was a hard way to earn one's keep, he scoffed and assured me he was on Social Security. I think he didn't want me to think he was broke. So I took his photo and gave him a few dollars for the privilege which he had a hard time accepting. But it is never something for nothing in the world of the honorable. He kept saying, "For real? For real?"

Yeah, for real, Pat. But I didn't give him the bizarre flesh 'n' fruit 'n' nut-paste Al-wich. That belonged to Shawn and the ages, and that's all there is to it.

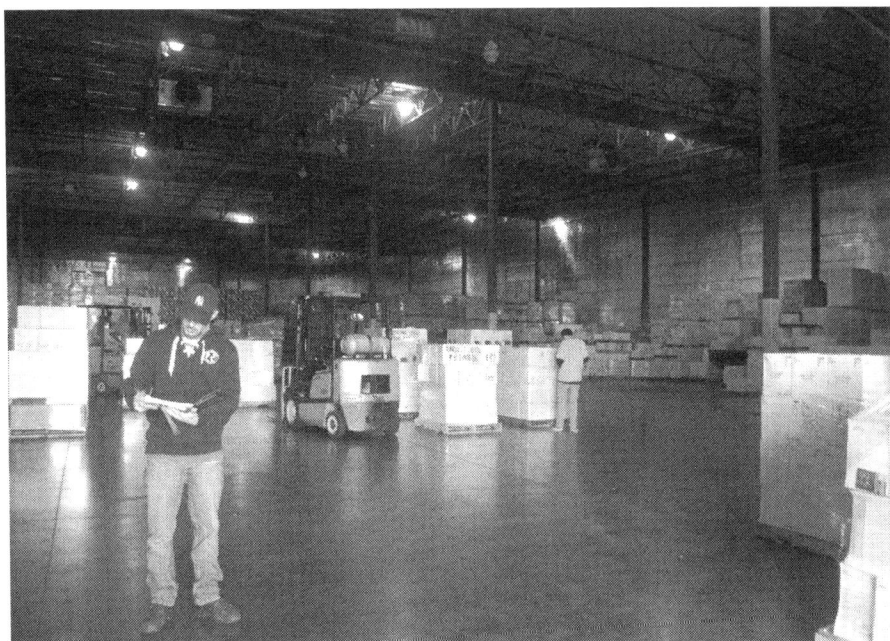

18. MICHAEL SCOTTO: NEVER THE WEAKEST LINK

In ten minutes it took me to scarf a Brooklyn Bomber sandwich (in honor of A2's hometown) at Cut the Mustard on E. Pine in Lodi, Michael Scotto took orders for the equivalent to a year's output for the average winery in the United States.

An order came in over his cell phone for 2300 mix-and-match cases, with shipping required in less than a week. Contrast that to 42% of wineries in the United States, where annual production is between one and five thousand cases, and you can imagine that in the course of a day, Scotto Family Cellars outdoes all but a small percentage of active winery's yearly sales. For Michael, this sort of business transaction was not all in a day's work, it was all in a lunch break's work.

Shortly after that, we headed over to Michael's nerve center—a single shelf in a break-room inside a cavernous wine warehouse where he has staked out the requisite territory for his trade tools: A laptop computer and a old printer on a stack of wine boxes.

Adjacent to his phone booth-sized operating footprint is Vanessa Manabat's office. She wears the lofty title of "Distribution Manager and Logistics Analyst" and is responsible for so many of the intricate threads that weave together the Scotto Family Cellars distribution dynasty that it would take a separate volume to list them. I bring her name into the story primarily because she is precisely the kind of individual that a lot of multi-million dollar corporations would not have taken a risk on: One of twelve kids from a low-income Stockton family, at 26, Vanessa has five children of her own ranging in ages from one to eleven. But the eye for detail that seems to suffuse most of A2's interactions holds as true for personnel as it does for broken drain grates in the winery, and when Vanessa came on board three years ago in an entry level position, he clearly recognized her potential.

"I worked every job in the warehouse at one time another," she says. "HR to packaging. I'm probably the only person here who can say that."

And yet, as is evident on every strata in every division of Scotto Cellars, the dividends paid by their faith in Vanessa far outstripped the risk; she may the poster child for a philosophy of trust: Despite a household overflowing with little Manabats, she has never once called in needing personal time for the family ("I have child care that doesn't ever let me down") and returns the trust in unshakable loyalty.

She is, according to Michael, an indispensible component in the flow of product that handles millions of gallons of wine a year.

Michael's own position in the flow chart began four years ago at a national sales meeting in San Francisco, when his father gauged his interest in joining the family business. At the time, Michael was capping nine years with Republic Document Management, a Dublin

(CA)-based process server that handled subpoenas throughout the Bay area and most of Central California. By the time of the come-to-Jesus moment, Michael had pretty much advanced about as high in that company as he was likely to go. He had, during his tenure, risen through the ranks, from a subpoena server to the dude who supervises subpoena servers. When you consider that this involved juggling precise process appointments over a vast territory among multiple crew members, A2 had kept a careful eye on this skill set his youngest son was developing, convinced that routing people was not drastically different than routing wine.

It took a couple of father/son heart-to-hearts to convince Michael Scotto to book passage on the family liner and a couple of years to prove out A2's instincts correct. Despite being in a job he now loves, surrounded by people he respects, Michael confesses that initially he had all sorts of butterflies: "I was intimidated, I admit it. Despite being from a wine family five generations deep, I really knew nothing about the industry—even less about the product."

And the unspoken vibe—at least, unspoken until I asked and Michael confirmed it—is that going into business where your two older brothers have already established themselves leads to a very intense family dynamic: First, you don't want to be the weakest link in the chain, and second, you want your department to outshine theirs, at least on some level. The idea of being a lodestar, in business ethics and personal integrity, is a common theme in all the conversations I had with the Scottos. But competition is not only a valuable tool in business, it is probably an indispensible one. When you toss in the natural rivalry between red-blooded siblings, a bond and about simultaneously, the result can be, but isn't always, a leap-frogging brand of quality.

In this case, it works. Like his siblings, he has worked the professional

Rubik's Cube and found the precise pattern that fulfills roles, fills holes and fuels goals within the convoluted family dynamic.

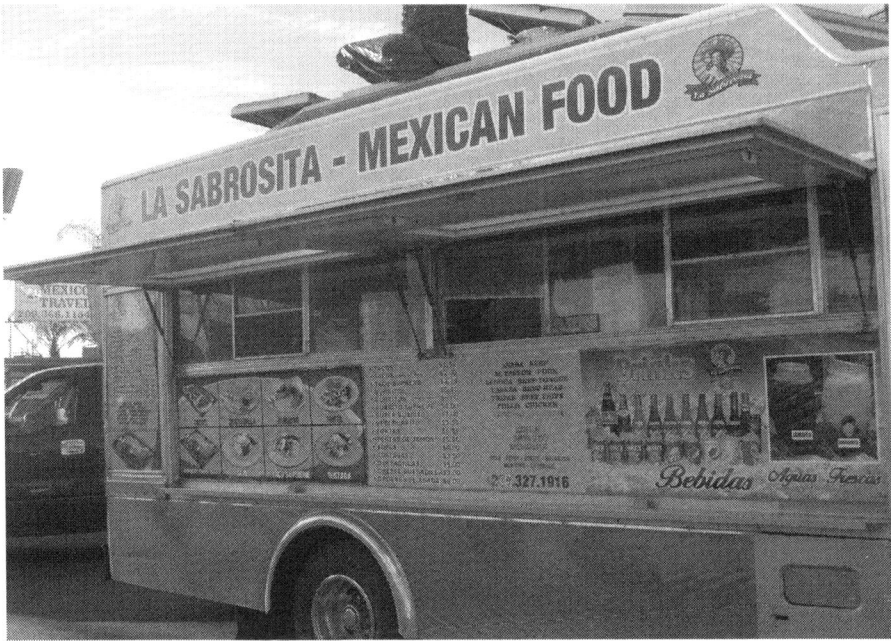

19. LA SABROSITA AND THE A&Ω OF A&W

Lodi is 500 miles from Mexico, but in many parts of town, you'd swear you are in a dusty maquiladora hamlet on the far side of the border. Entire sections are 100% Latino and stores speak Spanish exclusively. Street food here is in its own dimension—there are Mexican restaurants from Timbuktu to Katmandu, but the mobile taco trucks that are a cornerstone of every Lodi barrio and workplace do not have a real presence outside the American West. They hover at intersections, bookend festivals, and show up at midnight during grape harvest, which is typically done after dark to keep the grapes chilled before pressing.

Taco trucks are to Lodi what pretzels are to Midtown Manhattan: Elemental spirit.

If you put any stock into people's choice awards, La Sabrosita on the corner of E. Pine and N. Washington is a Michelin three-star, having proudly annihilated the competition during the Fourth Annual Taco

Truck Cook-Off on June 28, 2014, and although taco truck cook-offs have since come and gone like so many, La Sabrosita needs no further verification of raison d'être (in Spanish, razón de existir). You'll find the award prominently mentioned on the truck's side, right next to a menu that includes "beef tongue, beef heads and beef trips"—essentially, every part of a cow that gringos won't eat. Another favorite is al pastor (in the style of the shepherd), a taco from Central Mexico based on the shawarma spit-grilled meat brought by Lebanese immigrants. It's supposed to be lamb, but is almost always made from pork, conjuring up a pastoral image of Mexican hillsides dotted with shepherds dutifully tending their herds of pigs.

One assumes that the guts of taco truck patrons are made of sterner stuff than mine, but to watch the Hispanic hive buzzing around truck without coming across as a culture voyeur or a hopelessly lame white boy, so I had to order a couple of entry-level chicken tacos and do the requisite people watch while sitting at a picnic table and waiting for my order. La Sabrosita was so busy at 4:00 on a sunny Sunday afternoon that they were passing out numbers; mine was 53 and the sweating, squirming, hustling trio of truck cooks, who each had as much personal space as if they were preparing dinner in a shower stall, were only up to 40.

Mexicans everywhere have a certain stylistic distinction far apart from Caucasian couture; there's a penchant for flashy colors on women, giant belt buckles on men, and a nearly universal need to wear sunglasses in ways far more creative than the one in which God intended. As a primer course in this, if you want to go native, consider wearing your shades above the rim of your baseball cap, hanging from the nadir of the "v" in your v-neck t-shirt, draped across the top of your head, on the back of your head so you look like Cousin It—or worse, Guy Fieri—or the edgiest of all, dangling from your ears behind your head. I declined to even experiment with this last one in fear of the glasses falling off and breaking. How these strutting young cholos pull it off successfully is testimony to the power of muscle-coordinated fashion.

Numbers 40 through 52 represent several local social stratas; matronly types with impatient, explosively energetic kids touching puddles of spilled Jarritos and getting bitched at; young men in tight Adidas shirts whose lashy dates are waiting in the trucks or and diddle with cells phones; old guys with wrinkled mugs and cowboy hats and a sort of bland acceptance that long wait times are the fabric of reality. Staccato Spanish, lilting Spanish, mellifluous Spanish and beef head tacos are the thread that weaves this fabric together. And I'm the sore thumb taco, apparently: 40 through 52 were announced as cuarenta and cincuenta y dos, but when she came to mine, she called out a good old Americanese "fifty-three."

Taco trucks are a single branch in a food truck genealogy that extends back to the 17th century; mobile dining has been part of the mainstream since chuck wagons fed cattlemen and moveable canteens fed army troops. There is, therefore, no way to pin down when and where the first taco truck set up shop.

With the white bread root beer 'n' vanilla ice cream bastion A&W, the point of origin is as easy to pinpoint as the first trickle of water from northern Minnesota that becomes the mighty Mississippi River. The former issues from a small glacial lake in Clearwater County; the latter sits on the same corner of Lodi and Stockton, a block from I-99, that it has since before there was an I-99.

In June, 1919, A&W's 'A'—California entrepreneur Roy Allen— whipped up a batch of root beer using a formula he had purchased from a pharmacist in Arizona and began selling it from a roadside stand in Lodi. His timing could not have been better: In October of that same year, the Volstead Act went into effect, and sales of the other kind of beer, the real stuff, were prohibited.

In bone dry Lodi, figuratively and well as climatically, root beer filled a very big niche, as a thirst quencher if not a fire-starter.

At the original A&W Lodi stand, root beer went for a nickel a glass, and in part because of the basic innovation of 'cold mugs', it sold in such prodigious quantities that Allen soon expanded to Sacramento. In 1922 he took on a partner, A&W's 'W', Frank Wright, a former employee who was not related to Frank Lloyd Wright, as indicated by the impossibly kitschy-looking outlets shaped like giant beer barrels.

By Prohibition's end in 1933 there were 170 franchised A&W stores across the country, and despite the booze spigot being turned on once more, despite the Depression and despite World War II's strict sugar

136

rationing, the company continued to grow. The Golden Years for the brownish bevvie were after the war when the GI Bill permitted entrepreneurial veterans to get into the franchise game, and by 1960, there were over 2000 A&Ws, many of them cashing in on the car-hop craze of curbside service which they, in essence, had pioneered.

Although a hallmark of A&W's success has been consistency, and although the root beer formula is highly guarded and proprietary, the ground-zero A&W on the corner of Lodi and Stockton claims to use 'the original recipe' from 1919, which is probably unlikely since the active ingredient in sassafras is safrole, an oily phenylpropene that was banned in 1960 as a carcinogen.

Root beer is, for the record, a blend of ingredients as complex as any designer gin or Monk-made Chartreuse; it's rooted in sassafras root or sarsaparilla leaves, now synthetic, and probably was adapted from a Native American recipe. Additional flavor ingredients are what makes the formula a state secret; but a fair guess is that A&W's precious fluid, original recipe or extra legal, contains molasses, wintergreen, licorice and vanilla.

In fact, if this stuff is so good that Lodi is still bragging a century later, it makes absolutely no sense for me not to approach this dank, dunnish, dark-yet-frosty fluid with all the reverence of an Old Vine Zinfandel.

Fecal brown, but not in an off-putting way, the shivery confection opens with a bright nose reminiscent of Crest Pro-Health Whitening toothpaste, and interestingly, like the Russell Stover hard candy Root Beer Barrels you'd need a fluoride treatment to counteract; the mid-palate is pure sucrose rush, with notes of sugar beet and sugar cane and a soupçon of rock candy. The ice in the mug effectively kills any attempt at carbonation, and the finish is long, syrupy, sugary, cloying and molardegeneratingly sweet.

Both A&W and La Sabrosita are examples that show, more or less, how the other half dines in Lodi, so it was a logical progression to pick up a couple of beef head tacos and a carry-out root beer for Shawn the Alley Man, who returned from exile last night and has set up camp in his old digs by the power box. I have no idea what happened to Patrick the painter, but Shawn was nestled in among the mattresses, now with a computer screen set up on a milk crate. I figured he could hack into any of the local networks easily enough, and if not, I had no issue sharing a password. But of course, it was not a working computer; it was a prop like those trees in the old Twilight Zone episode where nothing in Centerville, a small town where no one lives, where houses are empty, telephones are stage sets, the food is plastic and the only train comes right back to Centerville.

So we sat in downtown Shawnville, ate funky tacos and lived a little underbelly reality in the midst of the fakery.

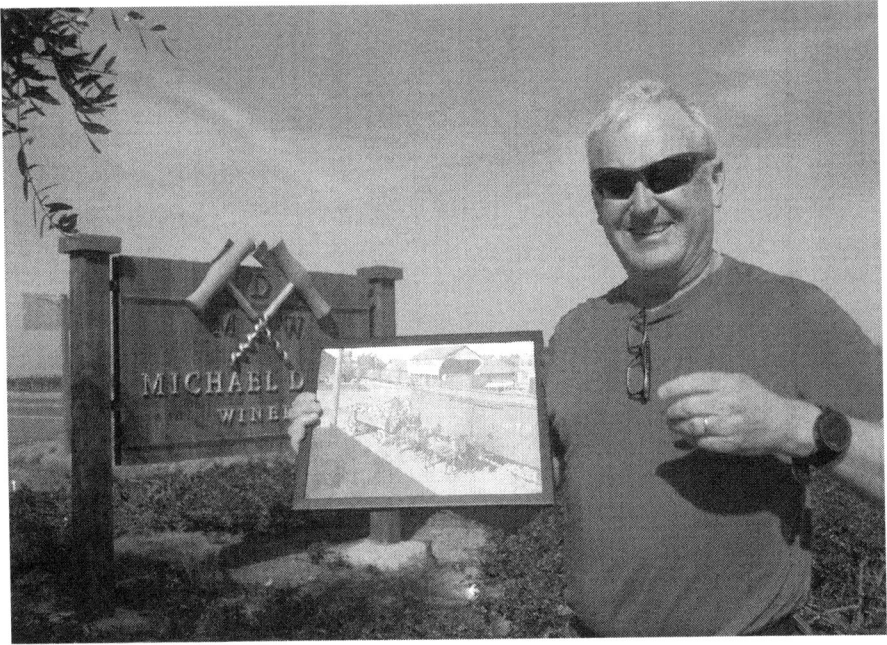

20. MICHAEL DAVID AND THE NAME THAT LAUNCHED A THOUSAND QUIPS

When it comes to Zinfandel puns on wine labels, what level of torture can you withstand? I mean, if an EMS technician asked you to describe your pain on an index that runs from 1 to 10? Is "Death To The Infidel" Zinfandel from Stillman Brown clever enough to earn a mere two or three? Does "Cardinal Zin" from Big House rank a solid 10 for acute, excruciating pain that prevents you from performing ADLs—activities of daily living? How about "Earth, Zin and Fire" from Jessie's Grove; Schellhardt's "Zynergy", or arguably the biggest laugh of all, Sutter Home White Zinfandel?

A lot of questions and a lot of debilitating discomfort—as a varietal, Zinfandel has a special affinity for bad jokes. So, what better place to ask them than at the point of origin, the source of the raging outflow, the place which is to bad Zin puns what Lake Itasca is to the Mississippi

River?

In 2002, David Phillips started in the fuss and left it to us. Today, he wears the broad, satisfied smile of a fellow who knows his place in the world. And he should—his DNA has been roughly the same place since the Civil War, and the only thing that has really changed is the number of acres he tills and the size of his bank account. And these are both smile-worthy notions.

I sat down with him in The Farm Café, a cozy nook on the long stretch of Kettlemen west of town; the café is adjacent to the tasting room which itself is a retro-fitted roadside produce stand from his family's earlier days—there is still a small produce section between the café and the wine bar. The Farm Café is known for serving the best fruit pies in town and I can vouch for the quality of the coffee as well: I drank three of them in the time it took David to appear.

This heel-cooling span may be construed as both deferential and requisite; after all, David Phillips is among the Lodi elite. He appeared warm and affable in the manner of somebody who has done hundreds of interviews; he settled in with the mien of a man who is comfortably busy but relaxed in a sort of imperious way, the monarch of all he surveys.

The monarchy includes one of the biggest and fastest-growing wineries in Lodi, recently named Winery of the Year at the 2016 Unified Wine & Grape Symposium, where the Phillips family was referred to as "the great California success story" by Jon Fredrikson, chairman of the symposium, the largest event of its kind in the western hemisphere.

Although David himself is not a particularly imposing gentleman—he's sort of down-home cuddly in a salt-of-the-earth-farmer sort of way, everything around him is imposing—his history, his farm, his reputation, his portfolio. In the course of my Lodi roving, I wanted to profile at least one winery exactly like Michael David; an old local family who have survived the ups and downs of farming and come up so far on top in a gazillion ways that they are both a template and testimonial for Lodi wine country as a concept.

They also produce the top-selling Zinfandel in the world, but I'll get to that.

The Phillips story begins with a lot of other names, family names, names from the matrilineality (as the genealogists say)—Harscheners, Maleys, Perrins. They all tried various combinations of produce, wheat to watermelon, following the market fluctuations like caribou after pastureland, or perhaps, like Ojibwe after caribou. In the end, whatever had the greatest return on the investment was the game plan: David Phillips said, echoing what Anthony Scotto III told me earlier in what is perhaps the simplest all-inclusive synopsis of the region:

"This is Lodi. We can grow anything we want."

For many years now, that has been grapes; first, Tokay, then wine grapes, and in 2016, that represents about 98% of what Phillips Farms grows. But its roots—no pun—are in a diversity of produce; David and his brother Michael grew up with tractors and fruit stands and stuff he's still proud to call "the sweetest corn around" while claiming bragging rights to having introduced the idea of heirloom veggies to Northern California, especially pumpkins and tomatoes. Over the generations, and there are now six, the Phillips clan found a market for their seasonal vegetables and fruits not only at the roadside stands established throughout the area, but at the slew of gourmet restaurants that had begun popping up throughout California in the last half of the 20th century. They grew plenty of wine grapes as well, but they went to the big boys, Gallo and Mondavi.

Then, in 1984, starting with a few acres of Syrah and Symphony—David and Michael Phillips founded their own winery (under the label Phillips) and began releasing a few hundred cases a year.

Here, Symphony deserves a time-out—this is a varietal that Michael David still produces as a stand-alone, and in fact, still wins gold and double gold awards for it, and yet I'd venture to guess that most wine people couldn't even tell you if it's a red grape or a white one (much less be able to pick it out of a line-up). In fact, it's white—a cross between Muscat of Alexandria and Grenache Gris—and grown primarily as a blending grape in Lodi and the nearby Sierra Foothills AVA.

But proof that it has the sinew and depth to own center stage Michael David's 2015 Symphony, filled with gentle, luscious flavors of honeysuckle, ginger and peach.

In 2000, the Phillips brand ran into legal difficulty when Phillips Wine & Spirits in Minnesota sued and won, and the Phillips brothers learned the hard way that not only was their own name proprietary, it wasn't their property—it was owned by some distribution company in St. Paul.

But surprisingly, as a middle finger to such silly lawsuits, it all worked out for the best: "The name change to Michael David turned out to be a gift," he told me. "Sales began to increase almost immediately; I have no idea why."

A large portion of that success was down to David's wild idea, in 2002, to combine the seven small-lot Zinfandels that he and Michael had been producing as individual wines into a single, all-inclusive blend. Having been a pair of pious parochial school kids, the brothers saw the humor potential in choosing a pun name for their new concoction that drew from their post-catechism embracing of a somewhat hedonistic lifestyle.

Thus, 7 Deadly Zins, the precursor to the a slew of pun wines that now spackle the wine shelves, was born, and is now—as David Phillips is proud to state—the best-selling Zinfandel in the world.

And that's the case in spite of the name, not because of it. It's a potent and portentous Zinfandel, reflecting Lodi spirit made manifest at the hands of a scion of one of the founding families. And David is not the slightest bit apologetic over the pun, over the palate, over the popularity.

Nor should he be: "According to Robert Parker, this is 90 point wine. It's big, for sure. Concentration is our goal. It tastes like Lodi, not like France or Italy or any place else. You're tasting what nature gives us: rich soils, abundant sunshine and hot days."

He shakes his head at locals who miss this all-encompassing reality, this soul-and-soil-defining gospel, this basic truth, both simple and complex, immediate and eternal.

And when David Phillips does that, he sounds more like a pundit than a punster:

"We're sitting in the greatest wine country in the world here; we grow more grapes in Lodi than Washington and Oregon combined, and as far as I'm concerned they're better than either one. But look around, you'll see vineyards neglected, almost like Old Vine Zin is so prevalent it's treated as an afterthought in places. I see vines being pulled out to lay concrete. It's the local economy; I get that, the search for the dollar. But we have to figure out how to convince people that vineyards have more value than strip malls."

21. THE CREEPIEST SPOT IN LODI

It's one o'clock in the morning and outside the window, the moon is bloated—a bulbous boil in the sky.

When you are just falling asleep, the way the sound of a distant train works is this: The whistle is as mournful as an owl's cry, evoking images of other places and other people with destinations beyond familiar horizons; it lulls you into dreamland filled with imagined stories of unique, exotic lives and a nagging, nostalgic melancholy.

When you are already asleep, the sound of a train a single block away works like this: You are jolted awake by the screech of an gargantuan angry beast—an entity bigger than life shrieking with inconceivable wrath at someone or something or no one at all; you are wrenched back to reality with a sense of horror in the pit of your gut and it takes a while before you realize that it is merely the San Joaquin connection, not a Talmudic shedim loosed from the bowels of Hell.

I assume that, given time, circadian rhythms would allow me to get used to it. I'm not there yet, which is why I'm wide awake at one in the morning, trying to accomplish something, anything, at my lonely keyboard while glancing over my shoulder at the fat, infernal moon.

I'm inside an old boarding house that has has been around since... well, nobody knows how long it's been around. And believe me, I checked. It used to be called the Del Rey Hotel, and nobody from the Lodi Historical Society had ever heard of it, nor did a Google search turn up a single hit. There are a couple of old photos on the wall that seem to be from around 1940; they show a somewhat featureless street lined with clunky Chryslers and pustulant Plymouths and a sign for Del Rey Rooms opposite the Lodi Theater and Rexall Drugs. Since the Del Rey building is directly across the street from the formerly swank Lodi Hotel, I am assuming that this place must have catered to a run-off crowd that couldn't afford the luxe, and I am assuming that a boarding house this old has many strange and squirrely stories hiding within it. People do desperate things inside boarding houses given enough time and booze and sufficient despair, and I felt wicked vibes inside the place from the moment I walked through the door.

What makes it creepier still is that I am the only person in the entire building.

The room on the ground floor is being gutted and refitted as a tasting room for Scotto Family Cellars, the good folks who spirited me across the country to write this book about Lodi. They stashed me comfortably in the old boarding house above the future tasting outlet—this upper story had already been refitted by a family who once lived up here.

They moved a while ago, for unknown reasons, and when they left, they took everything with them but the bed where I try to sleep and the

146

desk where I sit when sleep won't happen. The only thing thing missing when I wander down the long spooky boarding house hallway at one o'clock in the morning, where eight rooms snake off into their own dark and private microcosms, each door shut tightly and too horror-show to consider opening, is furniture and company.

You feel that the place is waterlogged with stories and that there's nobody left to tell them.

So on my last day here, I sought out Janice, a retired volunteer from the Historical Society, and she broke protocol and invited me to the town's museum, even though it was supposed to be closed and she was supposed to be at whatever work a person does when they say they are retired. Janice has lived in Lodi on and off since the 1940s, when the town was a whistle stop with a population of around ten thousand. I figured if anybody could shed some light on my haunted hotel, it was Janice.

So, what do you do when the place you go to find out about paranormal activity in your century-old boarding house is itself a sprawling, empty, eerie Victorian mansion built in 1900 and named... wait for it... Hill House? You bound up the boards and knock eagerly at the door like Eleanor Vance did in Shirley Jackson's iconic 1959 horror novel 'The Haunting of Hill House'.

As a Hill House caretaker, Janice is diminutive and precious; a small, white-haired historian who was eager to help track down any information on the Del Rey she had in the moldering archives of Lodi's records, and in fact, she began to pore through volumes of old directories and telephone books while I wandered through period room filled with faded wedding dresses hung on manikins, empty highchairs in forgotten kitchen nooks, spooky porcelain dolls in childrens' rooms, grinning and vacant, perhaps waiting for the return of daughters who have since grown old and died and are now themselves porcelain-colored bones in Lodi Memorial Park. Whether the tintype portraits that ring the halls of Hill House are more ghastly than most, I will not speculate, but they portray sunken-eyed, sober-faced specters whose silent vigil over the empty rooms is reminiscent of the opening lines of Shirley Jackson's 'The Haunting of Hill House':

"Hill House, not sane, stood by itself against its hills, holding darkness within; it had stood so for eighty years and might stand for eighty more. Within, walls continued upright, bricks met neatly, floors were firm, and doors were sensibly shut; silence lay steadily against the wood and stone of Hill House, and whatever walked there, walked alone."

There was, it turned out, virtually no mention of the Del Rey Hotel in any of the endless records; it was as if it never existed. Finally, a single ad turned up in an old Lodi newspaper from 1956 list Del Rey Rooms at the address, managed by a woman with the unlikely and unsettling name of Dorothy Rott.

But if I was unsuccessful in mining for Del Rey background, I did manage to unearth the true motherlode of Lodi's supernatural face and as it happened, I was standing in the parlor of the very crucible.

Hill House, on 826 Church Street, is haunted.

At least it is if you trust the professionals. Janice was happy to bring out a clipping from the Lodi News-Sentinel (the same paper with the Del Rey advertisement) from March 22, 2011 that chronicled the experiences of Kimberley Phillips of Lodi Paranormal Investigators over six post-midnight hours she spent within the house along with video cameras, recorders and EMF meters to detect fluctuations in electro-magnetic energy.

"I was blown away by it," she told Sentinel reporters. "I wasn't expecting anything like this."

The occurrences over that span of hours—which Phillips described as happening on a stormy night, itself an anomaly in Lodi—can be measured in varying degrees of inexplicability. In the master bedroom, the one with the wedding dresses, a man's voice was heard to utter, "Help me." In context of an impending marriage, that is perfectly understandable. Indeed, a woman's voice was heard to say, "Try my dress on," and a child replied, "Why, thank you." Within the disquieting silence of the doll room, a male voice referred to one of the investigators as "an idiot."

The corresponding secretary of Lodi's Historical Judy Halstead was initially skeptical, but having been the chaperone for the late night séance, she changed her tune. "A couple of things happened that made my jaw drop," she said.

Among them, and one that the docent Janice mentioned, involved a small container of face powder sealed within an acrylic display case. Halstead bore witness to Kimberley Phillips discovery of a small pile of the powder that had appeared without explanation beneath the case following the camp-out.

I couldn't track down Kimberley Phillips, even using a Ouija Board, but I did manage to find a guy named Tom Presler who runs a parallel universe of paranormal investigations, and although he had not been involved in the Hill House spook-fest, he did point out something that I guarantee most Lodi residents are not aware of:

Lodi, even before the town had been incorporated, and even before Steven Spielberg was born, was the site of the world's first Close Encounter of the Third Kind.

Fifty years before Roswell, in the November 19, 1896 edition of the Stockton Daily Mail, Colonel H.G. Shaw reported having seen a landed spacecraft near the Mokelumne River from which a trio of aliens emerged.

In his words:

"They resembled humans in many respects, but still they were not like anything I had ever seen. They were nearly or quite seven feet high and very slender. We were somewhat startled, as you may readily imagine, and the first impulse was to drive on. The horse, however, refused to budge, and when we saw that we were being regarded more with an air of curiosity than anything else, we concluded to get out and investigate. I asked where they were from. They seemed not to understand me, but began – well, 'warbling' expresses it better than talking. Their remarks, if such you would call them, were addressed to each other, and sounded like a monotonous chant, inclined to be guttural. I saw it was no use to attempt a conversation, so I satisfied myself with watching and examining them. They seemed to take great interest in ourselves, the horse and buggy, and scrutinized everything very carefully."

He also offered this as verification:

"Were it not for the fact that I was not alone when I witnessed the strange sight I would never have mentioned it at all. I went out to Lodi in company with Camille Spooner, a young man recently arrived from Nevada."

The real Colonel H.G. Shaw was the officer portrayed by Matthew Broderick in 'Glory'.

Tom Presler also directed me to a copy of the San Francisco Bee from the day before, November 18, 1896, in which residents reported seeing mysterious lights in the sky at an estimated 1,000-foot elevation. Some witnesses reported the sound of singing as the craft passed overhead and a man named E.L. Lowrey claimed that he heard a voice from the craft issuing commands to increase elevation. San Francisco is a hundred miles from Lodi, and by conventional means of locomotion, excluding high speed rail or flying saucer; there was a day's travel time between the two cities. The likelihood of statistical coincidence for these two juxtaposed accounts I leave to math majors.

Beyond his work in the paranormal, Presler is the founding father of the Lodi Zombie Walk, now in its eighth consecutive year. On the Saturday before Halloween, hundreds of undead wannabes from all over Northern California dress up in rags and prosthetics and take over downtown and various participating wineries in a city-wide stumble rumble.

If possible, on October 29th of this year, I'd like to bring the whole thing around full circle and have the Zombie Walk stop at the Lodi Memorial Garden and see if anyone can summon the spirits of Nellie Hill and Dorothy Rott. They left behind some loose ends and it's high time they tied them up, if for no reason other than posthumous posterity.

Shirley Jackson's ghosts may walk alone, but with Presler's gang, there is no reason why Lodi ghosts should have to.

22. A2: THE SYNDICATE OF FATE

For me, the toughest chapter in this book to write, yet the one I most looked forward to writing while measuring the constituent words most carefully and my approach with the most circumspection, probably should not have been written at all: The gentleman who it is all about asked me not to.

He told me as much at a hastily arranged sit-down, and it was pretty unsettling, because by then, the man in question—Anthony Scotto II, father of the brood whose various companies are requisite layers in the massive Scotto cake, and thus, this story—had become the fulcrum, if not the focus, of my Lodi experience.

The cease-and-desist request happened within in the windowless cloister of Cluff, the Scotto family's name for their east Lodi location. One morning, about half way through my stay, A2 summoned me, and—brows slightly knit, expression vaguely grizzled, eyes showing the sort of

153

slow-burn smolder that only an Italian from Brooklyn can truly muster (a look that doesn't necessarily say "Let's do business" as much as "I mean business")—asked that I not include a chapter on him.

"This should be the story of my children's successes, not mine."

The problem was, Starstruck in Lodi Again is not intended to be a book about anyone's individual success; it's supposed to be a still life from Drawing 101. It is a compendium of charismatics, a potpourri of personalities, a variety of viewpoints, and when it comes to success, nobody does it alone. Some folks succeed "because of" and some people succeed "in spite of," but few people succeed without some form of input, positive or negative, from those that surround them.

As interesting as the Scotto kids are, their story would be half-unwritten without a literary nod to the foibles, fortunes, faculties and feelings of their sire.

So, I explained in as respectful, but unyielding tone as I could muster that the request would have to be denied. A2 needs his chapter for posterity, I need it as a nexus and I believe his kids need that chapter as an expression of family honor.

There's a hackneyed expression, "Just do it and let the chips fall where they may."

Okay, then. I did and here is where they fell:

On the Scotto Family Cellars label, there's a monochromatic silhouette of a fellow with a smart, efficient-looking cap and a push-cart full of wine jugs. It looks somewhat generic, but in fact it is quite personal: It depicts Anthony Scotto I, who in 1940 began selling jugs of his father's homemade red wine, pushing them door-to-door on a cart. Like most wine that burbled up from immigrant basements, this was rustic, satisfying and inexpensive stuff filled with grapey acids and earthy residue, and in any case, for the old man with the recipe, Dominic Scotto, who had emigrated to Brooklyn in 1903 from Ischia—a volcanic island in the Tyrrhenian Sea of the coast of Naples—winemaking was strictly a cottage industry. He worked as a ship caulker at the nearby docks, and in 1934, opened a small, post-Prohibition liquor store on Court Street in Carroll Gardens, and it's still in operation to this day. But the itinerant jug-selling was strictly the enterprise of his sons, and in 1948, they branded their product Villa Armando, and today, it is one of the oldest wine labels in the country. As to total production to date, the family likes to toss around a figure of 200 million glasses.

I say "to date" because in 2016, the brand is alive and well. But there was a time when the business failed and the IRS swooped in and Anthony, then an employee of his father, found himself out of work. A series of clever maneuvers and canny gambles that brought Villa Armando back from the grave, and none of them, as the story goes, were the old man's doing.

"He was a good father, but a lousy leader," says A2, using a phrase to describe his father I heard from him so often over my Lodi month that it became sort of a litany.

Litanies or otherwise, A2 is a fun guy to listen to. Although he moved to California at 18, his Brooklyn accent remains acute, preserved in amber, so pure and unabashedly Noo Yawk that it is a casting director's beau ideal. The mechanics of this particular speech pattern are almost as interesting as the pronunciations—the pursed lips, the pushed-forward tongue, the interdental fricatives, the alternating pitches, the hand gestures. A2's dialect is midway between street Italian and Yiddish, in which single syllable 'a' and 'o' are replaced with double syllables 'aww-uh' (so that "Talk about coffee" becomes "Taww-uhk about caww-uhfee"), and a word-ending 'r' is harder to find than an egg cream in Lodi.

What I did manage to find in Lodi was a couple of other native New Yorkers who moved to California and promptly lost all traces of Big Apple-ese, and when I asked them why—and how—they all had the same response: They were self-consciousness, rightly suspecting that their garish, nasally East Coast honking pigeonholed them as strangers in a strange land. The point is, for the most part, it did, and so they forced themselves to drop the argot and the localisms, pull back their tongues and converse in bland, rather featureless Californian.

Not so, Anthony Scotto II. Then as now, it's not that he doesn't care or that he's immune from self-consciousness; far from it. But the stand-up quality that had him sit me down and insist (fortunately, unsuccessfully) that I leave him out of the Lodi story is also demonstrated in his loyalty to the stuff of which he made—the sinews and seasoning of his background. He doesn't see his roots as a liability and certainly, his heritage is not something he wants to gloss over or hide, and his Brooklyn accent—as sharp and musical and acute as when he was a street kid selling illegal fireworks on Canal Street—remains as a barometer of his personality, a gauge of his character.

So does his van. A cliché in New York and California and most points between is that when a street kid makes good, the first thing he buys is an expensive land barge—the requisite symbol of conspicuous consumption. A2 may have owned his share of hot wheels over the years, but today he drives a beat up cream-and-rust colored step van from somewhere in the last century. It's filled with his life's detritus—wine bottles, paperwork, gas station caww-uhfee cups—one gnarled hand grips a worn steering wheel while the other goes through a steady series of gestures, his handsome, ethnic Italian face never strays from the road—he treats his van with kid's gloves, never exceeding the speed limit (in my experience) and pulling over to the shoulder without complaint if some impatient Californian behind him figures he's Sunday driving.

He loves that van as much as Sammy Johns ever did (if for totally different reasons) and his kids have offered repeatedly to pitch in and buy him a new one. And he has just as repeatedly refused the offer. In fact, one of first conversations I had with A2 was when he informed me, in no uncertain terms, that if worse ever came to worse (and however I might interpret that) he would be more than capable of living out of that van. So, I interpreted "worse" as meaning him losing everything precious to him except the van, and that would be—first and foremost—his wife, Gracie.

When writing a basic profile of a complicated individual, trying to capture a multiplex personality in a handful of words, I have a tendency to look for bite-sized pieces. Embodiments. In A2, I found first, his patriotism to his former New York hood, and second, his battered van, but above all, his attitude toward his wife (some might toss in the old-school adjective "long suffering") of nearly 40 years.

To say that he reveres her is an understatement; I have met men—many of them of Italian descent—who built pedestals big enough to accommodate both their mothers and their wives, and generally in that order. This would not be the one A2 builds; his descriptions of his mother are eerily similar to some of the conversations Tony Soprano had with Dr. Malfi, and I have no reason to doubt their veracity. Mom didn't care for Gracie on principal (she is Hispanic, which, in the estimation of an overbearing Italian mother from Brooklyn, makes her a Rican—Puerto Rican, Costa Rican, Mexi-rican, doesn't matter) and in any case, didn't think she was a suitable match for her youngest son. Anthony, barely more than a kid at the time, defied her, and a lot of the conversations we had centered around the validity of his defiance, his choice. Gracie occupies a rarified throne in the Scotto kingdom, and A2 seems to exude a Wayne 'n' Garth sense of "I'm not worthy."

Is he worthy? Gracie thinks so, and thus, to him (and by default, to us), no other opinion should matter.

The kids feel the same way about their mother, and with slightly less need to prove and maintain their worth. Gracie is a small women, feisty but eminently soft-spoken, down-to-earth and as eminently proud of her Mexican heritage as her husband is of his Italiano blood. She embraced me from the moment we met, with nothing to prove to me and no apparent concerns about what I might write about her, only a slight bafflement that I'd care to write about her at all.

But she adds precise and judicious seasoning to this story with a smile, happy to share: When she first met Anthony Scotto II, he was dating her best friend and she found him callous and brash and way too New Yorkish for her quiet, rural California tastes. Plus, he was a drummer in a hardcore metal band that played Metallica covers and once opened for Pantera, or maybe they played Pantera and opened for Metallica;

I forget. In any case, he was not her type at all—he was flashy, and she was sedate, studious and serious. But he was persistent, and in time, after the relationship with her friend sizzled out, she yielded just enough to recognize that Anthony had another side. She began to see a manifestation of his focus and drive in his serious attitude toward music in a band that partied hearty and loved the rock star life, and that impressed her. Along with the gut-level affability that bubbles just below his surface, this was enough to convince her to give him a romantic shot, and (other than a chunk of time when A2 was MIA, a time which he is perfectly willing to discuss, and which ultimately leads to his feelings that he is, today, far luckier than he deserves to be) the relationship has been on solid footing ever since.

Nowhere is this more obvious than during massive, old school Scotto family dinners, where everything radiates from a sprawling spread—a gioia della tavola that can be handled as effectively by a pretty Latina from Central California as a big-boned mamma from Brooklyn. Of course, there are some cultural concessions, and the distillation of the primary Italian directive mangia, mangia is pendulous with pasta and salumi, voluminous salads, simple and fresh, complex and preserved, everything accompanied by the lifeblood that, if indispensible at any Italian table, is—if such a thing were possible—magnified to even greater importance at this one: Wine.

And, at a gathering of a family who, let's be honest, could afford to stack the sideboard with Sassicaia and Valdiclava, the omnipresence of the wine that's pictured on the label of the Scotto Cellars being tugged along by a man in a delivery cap—a man who shares DNA with everyone at the table except the spouses.

This hand drawn silhouette has no face, which is just as well. His character is anonymous to the average wine drinker who picks up a bottle in Duluth, or Chicago, or Nashville, or Cleveland, but everybody at the family table here knows exactly who he is: He is the Scotto paradigm as envisioned by the current patriarch, Anthony Scotto II. He's the man that A2 strives to be every day, the man that he hopes his sons and his grandsons, his daughters and his granddaughters, will strive to be throughout each of their own daily increments: Self-sustaining, self-confident, self-directed and above all, imbued with a sense of self-worth.

As A2 knows better than anyone, valuing one's self does not always go with the territory of success, and this is one of the reasons why he treats entry-level employees with the same respect as the CEO. This particular attitude, more than the wine, more than the heritage, more than the nostalgia, more than the van, defines the Scotto ideal, and represents to me, after my month in the soul of it, not only what Anthony Scotto II is striving for, but what Lodi - beginning to find a place on the stage - is striving for.

On long drives through the Lodi hinterland, A2 and I had many discussions about honor and blood and responsibility; far more than we did about wine. I have never met a man more devoted to his family who was simultaneously as cognizant of the fact that their existence is a matter of chance, of serendipity, not pre-destiny. Their successes, like his own, are the culmination of luck and labor, the synthesis of circumstance, accidents of birth, a syndicate of fate: Michael the Logistics man, Paul the Craftsman, Anthony the Salesman, Natalie the Disseminator, two more daughters who currently play no role in the family business but command equal real estate in his heart, and most of all, Gracie, the adhesive that binds them all together.

Other than their genes, the Scotto kids are not especially iconic among the staff and they understand that, and demonstrate it, as well as their father. They are a family that chose to be together by desire, not by edict.

A2 introduced me to a number of local men who the Scottos have encouraged, empowered and retained despite the odds, despite slip-ups both legal and professional: These fellows are, in the main, a motley crew. But appearances can be deceiving; temperaments cannot.

According to A2, one thing unites them:

"They are each instilled under an umbrella of respect and have each developed a foundation of loyalty; they're subjected to peer-pressure, self-filtering behavior, given space to monitor their own work. We insist on making them feel relevant and appreciated."

"They may look like simple people," A2 says in the most all-encompassing statement of our entire time together, "but they act like blessed men."

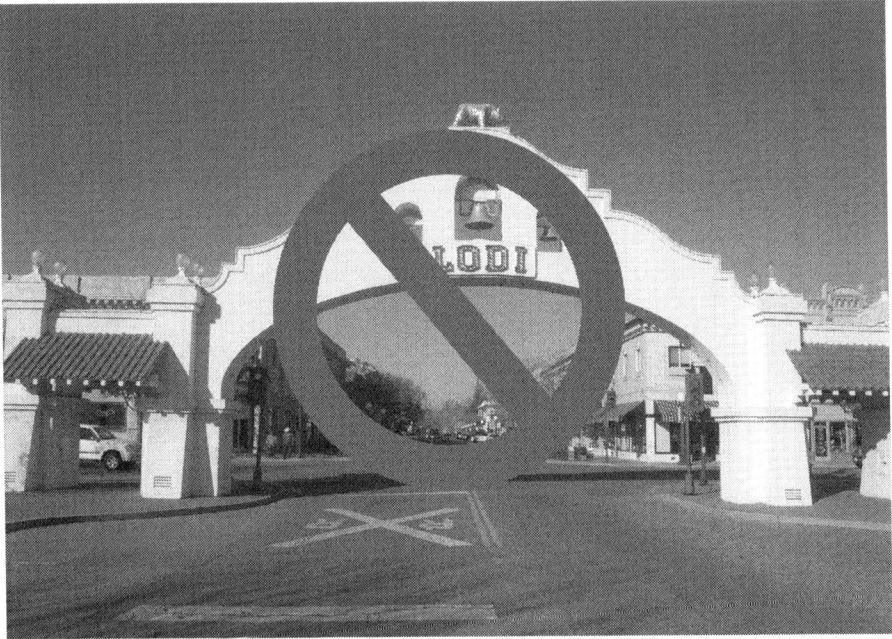

23. HOME BEACONS: LEAVING LODI

I knew I was on a Detroit-bound plane when the 1st grader in the adjacent seat, watching his father play video games on an iPhone, said, "I want to see you play that one where everybody's head explodes."

Any time I spend a month outside my drab hometown—especially in the middle of winter—I have to hit refresh on that mental tab that can deal with the inevitable reactions I get when I mention Detroit by name. This ranges from awkward silence to looks of sympathy similar to those I'd get if I just mentioned my grandmother died. Seizing the brass ring was the good ol' boy in Atlanta who simply shrugged and said, "Guess ever'body's got to be from somewhere."

Still, people from Lodi must get awfully sick of strangers saying, "Guess you're stuck in Lodi again, huh?" as though they're the first yukster in the history of humanity to ever make that witty connection. They will, I hope, forgive me for making one in my book title—the last one I will ever feel obligated to rely on. That's because to me, Lodi revealed something of her true temperament, something as near to the surface as those legendary old-time groundwater water tables and as deep as the alluvial loam. Lodi's lucid landscapes and clement climes were correctly assessed both by sixth-generation farmer David Phillips and by fourth-generation vintner Anthony Scotto III: "This is Lodi. We can grow anything we want."

Nobody to me seemed particularly stuck in Lodi; on the contrary, I found people who had moved to Lodi from all over the United States. The price of real estate may be the uptick, but you can still buy top-quality vineyard acres here cheaper than nearly anywhere else you'd want to settle. John Fogerty used Lodi to symbolize a sad, desolate, lonely California town where one might find oneself at a career's dead end, but in fact he claims today that he simply liked the rhythm of the name. He insists that it was nothing personal.

The only time I felt stuck during my whole Lodi layover was in a rare traffic jam on I-99, and even then it was heading into town, not out.

For a mainstream wine lover, Lodi in February is as close to ideal as anywhere I have ever been. Fat grapes trembling on vines in early autumn is a photo op, no doubt, but Old Vine Zinfandel is a sculptor's paradise in the winter—each scraggled old vine is writhing inside its own personality, and you don't so much take a picture of a vine as a portrait. The wines are phenomenal, and there is never a wait in any tasting room—in fact, they'll be delighted to see you. And if you ask if they charge you a tasting fee, they'll look at you like you just asked for some crack cocaine or told them you were from Detroit.

And the weather, if you are into exquisite weather, is exquisite. In a month, it sort of rained once; the rest of the time was sunshine and lollipops—blue skies, springtime balmy with temperatures between 65° and 75°. I may have lucked out between El Niño onslaughts; that was never made entirely clear. But it's easy to get lulled into a sense of complacency in this environment. It's easy to forget that in Detroit, in February, doing anything at all outside is a Herculean task. Putting on your winter gear is like donning a millstone. Walking to your car is an atmospheric albatross. Backing out of the driveway? Forget about it.

Natalie Scotto admitted that she forgets the entire country doesn't bask in such bucolic beauty during the opening months of the year. Paul Scotto is more concerned with early bud break leading to an early ripening, and that ever-warmer winters might allow certain soil pests to survive when they'd otherwise have died and Michael has too much on his logistics plate to think about it one way or the other. A3 is like one of those pinballs beneath the rapid-fire manipulation of The Who's deaf, dumb and blind kid, bouncing from appointment to meeting to lunch date with frenetic energy—he wouldn't let a blizzard cramp his style in any case.

But A2 gets it. Brooklyn born and to-the-corner bred, thick with city smarts and his incessant drive to tackle Category 4 whatevers, hurricanes to snowstorm, he seeks out life's hurtles and promptly vaults them. And you never get the impression it's to show off—on the contrary, it's the opposite: His forward momentum toward personal tsunamis in imagined oceans is the metabolism of a sea creature that needs to keep moving to survive. It's only in retrospect—looking in the rearview mirror to see the mountain ranges already crossed—that a little pride sets into A2's tone, and even then, it's is not an aggrandizement pin to wear on the lapel, but in context of the comfortable life he's brought to Gracie (after a couple of missteps) and the wealth of opportunity he's provided his children.

For me, A2 can be defined within three traits combined—modesty, strength and family-first—and seasoned with a street grit I associate with Brooklyn, with Chicago, with Detroit, with intense urban milieu that have at least one thing in common: Bitter and brutal Februarys.

If you are open to it, these sorts of months can build up more sensitivity than scar tissue; they can instill in one love for balmy days pure, intrinsic appreciation, not inurement to their value. Spring is never as sweet without acknowledging life's other side; the side where backing out of the driveway is a pain in the ass.

It certainly snows in Brooklyn, and when A2 reminisces about his childhood there, his words are filled with substance, his memories with subtext. And in the end, despite the warm California sun, when the last bottle on his watch has been capped, when the kids are established and the game is finished, it's easy to understand why he insists he will return to those streets. That's where the touchstones are, not in Lodi. He seems to be in his element wherever he goes, primarly because he creates his own element wherever he goes. But in, Brooklyn, I suspect, I could find the element that created him.

"In the end, I'll move back," he confessed. "I have to. Those are my roots."

Upon winning the Battle of Zela in 47 BCE, his countryman Julius Caesar spoke to the Roman Senate and described his conclusive victory in a phrase that has echoed through the millennia: 'Vini, vidi, vici.'

It means, of course, "I came, I saw, I conquered." Consider that Anthony Scotto II will finally bring another imperative to the table, turning the literary tricolor into a tetracolon:

"Redii domum": "And then I went back home."

In the end, we should all be so fortunate, so assertive and so victorious.

33662023R00107